# MOVING UP
*in the*
# MUSIC BUSINESS

## JODI SUMMERS

ALLWORTH PRESS
NEW YORK

05   04   03   02   01   00            5   4   3   2   1

Published by Allworth Press
An imprint of Allworth Communications
10 East 23rd Street, New York, NY 10010

Cover design by Douglas Design Associates, New York, NY

Page composition/typography by SR Desktop Services, Ridge, NY

Library of Congress Cataloging-in-Publication Data
Summers, Jodi.
    Moving up in the music business / Jodi Summers.
        p.     cm.
    Includes bibliographical references and index.
    ISBN 1-58115-061-X (pbk.)
    1. Popular music—Vocational guidance.   2. Music trade—Vocational guidance.   I. Title.
ML3795.S8697   2000
780'.23'73—dc21                                          00-033216


Printed in Canada

*To everyone who has tried to
make their dreams reality*

# *Table of*
# Contents

# Thanks to . . .

Keith Abbott, president of Abbott Promotions
Kathy Acquaviva, CEO of the public-relations firm Kathy Acquaviva Media
Gregg Alexander, producer, former frontman for the New Radicals
Marco Barbieri, vice president and general manager of Century Media Records
Tom Barsanti, senior vice president and general manager of Jeff McClusky
    & Associates
John Bates, cofounder and evangelist for BIGWORDS.com
Anthony Berman, multimedia and entertainment law attorney with
    Idell, Berman & Seitel, in San Francisco
Janet Billing, management for the Breeders, Lisa Loeb, Cibo Matto, and the
    Lemonheads
Len Blum, screenwriter; wrote the script for the Howard Stern film
    *Private Parts*
Hanna Bolte, senior director, media relations, West Coast BMI
Jon Bon Jovi, multiplatinum rock star and all-around media icon
Gary Bongiovanni, editor-in-chief of Pollstar
David Bowie, singer/songwriter, visionary artist
Bill Boyd, lighting technician
Danny Bramson, soundtrack producer
Bryn Bridenthal, head of publicity for DreamWorks Records
Kathy Callahan, senior director of western regional sales at Windham Hill
    Records
Nancy Camp, Drastic Measures, Inc. in Georgia
Vince Castellucci, senior director of licensing at the Harry Fox Agency
Mark S. Chasan, founder of emusic, composer/arranger, and much more!
JC Chasez, one of the mega-popular rock dreams in 'N Sync
Bob Chiappardi, president and CEO of Concrete Marketing
James Citkovic, Countdown Entertainment Management
Taylor Clyne, founder of Which? Records
Laura Cohen, manager of publicity for Virgin Records
Ted Cohen, executive vice president of Digital Music Network, Inc., part of
    DMN Communications and Webnoize
Paul D. Colford, author of *Howard Stern: King of All Media*
Miles Copeland, CEO, ARK 21 Records
Chris Cornell, singer/songwriter, former frontman for Soundgarden
Chuck D, the lyrical terrorist who leads the rap group Public Enemy,
    and MP3 advocate
Joe Daniels, drummer for Local H
E. J. Devonale, Hard Head Management
Chris Douridas, A&R for DreamWorks Records

George Drakoulias, staff producer and A&R executive for American Recordings

Jack Endino, producer of hundreds of Seattle punk records, including discs for Nirvana, Mudhoney, and Skin Yard

Sully Erna, vocalist for Godsmack

Ahmet Ertegun, founder, cochairman, and co-CEO of the Atlantic Records Group

Earl Falconer, bass player for UB40

Joey Fatone, Jr., one of the mega-popular rock dreams in 'N Sync

Tony Ferguson, A&R for Interscope Records

Fieldy, bass player for Korn

Vic Firth, timpani player with the Boston Symphony and timpani mallet manufacturer

Flavia, guitarist with the Swedish band Drain STH

Phil Frazier, manager/shopping agent

JJ French, president of French Management Enterprises

Tom Freston, MTV Networks chairman and CEO

Robert Fripp, singer/songwriter, music visionary, founder of Discipline Global Mobile

Marc Geiger, cofounder of ARTISTdirect, a triple-faceted entertainment venture

Gary Gersh, copresident of >EN Music Group

Richard Gotterrer, CEO of Sol 3 Records and Orchard Distribution

Lucas Graves, analyst for Jupiter Communications

Jim Griffin, chief executive at OneHouse

Sammy Hagar, solo singer, songwriter, and guitarist

Jonathan Hahn, president of MusicMarc, a copy protection software company

Jim Heath, founder of the Reverend Horton Heat

Brian Herb, founder of Mother of All Music Records

Dexter Holland, lead singer for the Offspring

Ice-T, rap artist, president of Body Count Records

Dan Ingram, disc jockey once known as the sound of afternoon-drive radio in New York City; currently with WCBS-FM (101.1) in New York City

Jimmy Iovine, cofounder of Interscope Records

David Javelosa, composer, producer, and technology evangelist for Yamaha game developer relations

David S. Kennedy, Sr., independent songwriter located at *www.wserv.com/~dkennedy*

David Kessel, president of IUMA/Offline Records

Tim Klahs, SFX investor relations director

Abbey Konowitch, executive vice president at MCA Records

Tommy Kotchik, roadie for the group Bedford

David Krebs, president of Krebs Communications management

Iara Lee, founder of Caipirinha Music

Michael Leventhal, technology/new media partner, Wolf, Rifkin & Shapiro, LLP

David Lowery, member of the Virgin Records band Cracker

Mike Luba, founder of Madison House Tour Promotions

Scott Lucas, singer/guitarist for Local H

Jill Mango, director of publicity for Wind-Up Records

Duff McKagan, solo artist, former bass player for Guns N' Roses

Peter Mench, cochairman of Q Prime Management

Sloane Smith Morgan, founder of the Law Office of Sloane Smith Morgan, an arts and entertainment law firm with offices in Berkeley and San Francisco

Doug Morris, chairman and CEO of Universal Music Group

Mark Mothersbaugh, founder of Mutato Muzika and DEVO

Dave Mustaine, singer/songwriter; founder of Megadeth

Gary Nicholson, songwriter, producer

Scott Nordvold, pyrotechnics expert and stagehand

Oded Noy, musician and composer

Paul Orescan, vice president and marketing director for MCA Records

Donald Passman, attorney with Gang, Tyre, Ramer & Brown, and author of *All You Need to Know About the Music Business* (June 1997, Simon & Schuster)

Joey Peters, drummer and percussionist for Grant Lee Buffalo

Brian Reed, associate manager at Borman Entertainment; production/tour manager for James Taylor

Vince Reese, president of Sasquatch Entertainment

Vernon Reid, songwriter, guitarist, and founder of Living Colour

Bob Rice, synthesizer programming and computer music applications

Ken Rich, owner of Rich Sounds, which does restoration of antique keyboards

John Richards, scoring mixer

Keith Richards, guitarist/cofounder of the Rolling Stones

Michael Robertson, CEO of MP3.com

Alicia Rose, vice president, head buyer, general manager, slave driver, and queen for NAIL Distribution

Larry Rosen, chairman and CEO of N2K and Music Boulevard/CDNow

Michael Rosenblatt, senior vice president, A&R, MCA Records

Tim Rozner, tour production manager

Jason Rubenstein, composer, texturalist

Mark Rydell, Academy Award–nominated director

Mitch Schneider, president of the MSO Organization

James Schureck, director of new media for Jeff McClusky & Associates

Bud Scoppa, vice president of A&R for the Sire Records Group

Andy Secher, editor of *Hit Parader* Magazine

Jean Segendorph, a partner in PolySutra Entertainment in New York City

John Silva, manager representing such top rock acts as the Foo Fighters, the Beastie Boys, Beck, Rancid, and Sonic Youth

Owen Sloane, entertainment industry attorney

Erik Smith, rigger

Will Smith, multitalented actor/rapper

Paul Stanley, cofounder of Kiss

Scott Stapp, singer/songwriter for Creed

Roger Stein, founder of Iguana Records

Howard Stern, king of all media

Sheryl Stewart, disc jockey for Air 1 Christian stations

Steve Summers, vocalist for Sprung Monkey

Al Teller, founder of AtomicPop.com, former chairman/CEO of MCA Music
Entertainment Group, and president of labels such as Columbia
Records and United Artists Records

Trish Thompson, member of Glass Candle Grenade

Mark Tremonti, guitarist for Creed

Steve Tyler, Aerosmith lead singer

Lars Ulrich, drummer for Metallica

Rod Underhill, Esq., director of business affairs for MP3.com

Edward Van Halen, guitarist for Van Halen

Tom Viscount, lead singer and the primary writer for the band Viscount

Matthew Wilder, film composer

John Williams, film composer

Marilyn Williams, account manager at Ad Personnel Headhunters

Peter Wiltz, keyboard technician for the Rolling Stones

Lajon Witherspoon, vocalist for Sevendust

Jonathan Wolff, TV composer

Steve Wood, tour manager for Megadeth

DJ David X, club DJ

Dave Yeskel, vice president of sales for the Windham Hill Group of Labels

Rob Zombie, recording artist and founder of Zombie A Go-Go Records

# Section 1

## The Basics: Taking Care of Business

# ADVANCING:

## *You <u>Can</u> Get There from Here*

The members of the multiplatinum, Grammy Award–winning band 'N Sync were asked to give advice to someone wanting to succeed in the music industry. Two of the five members responded:

JOEY FATONE, JR.: "Practice, practice, practice!"

JC CHASEZ: "Don't be discouraged easily. Hard work always pays off. Stay focused."

You've got a burgeoning career in the music business, but you want more—more access, more power, more responsibility, more money. Or maybe your career is not moving as fast as you want it to, or you're making money but not doing what you want to be doing. Maybe you're tired of touring, or you want more control over your destiny. You're dead-ended and want to move up in another area, but you don't see how. Where do you go from here?

Whether you are a technician on the road, a performer, a secretary, or a salesperson, the music industry offers myriad possibilities for career growth and change. *Moving Up in the Music Business* will show you how to assess, develop, and utilize the skills you already have to open the windows to new professional horizons.

## What Does the Music Business Mean to You?

"The music industry is basically helping to translate an artist's visions into a career," declares Jill Mango, director of publicity for Wind-Up Records. "It's a balance between art and commerce."

For many of us in the music business, our work is a means of having fun, making money, and traveling the world at someone else's expense. Basically, it's a carte blanche to fame, fortune, and opportunity—if you play it properly. If you don't play it properly, you can wind up destitute and out of the industry within weeks. As the music business is high on glamour and visibility, it's a popular career choice. But if you're going to succeed, you've got to play the game better and smarter than anybody else.

"You've got to continually think one step ahead of the other people," advises Andy Secher, editor of *Hit Parader* magazine. "The music business is like a giant game of chess. Most of the people in this industry are in it to meet famous people and hang out. If those are your goals, you're going to be extremely limited in your opportunities."

Getting a good break is more a matter of good fortune than anything else. It's a function of that elusive ability to be in the right place at the right time and flashing a smile at the right person.

Andy Secher owes his success to luck. "When I came out of college, I found out I was one credit short of getting my degree in journalism. I had to take an independent study course, which was working for a local newspaper," he recalls. "I parlayed that newspaper column, which was in an indie newspaper in New York called *Our Town,* into a nationally syndicated newspaper column, using the facilities of the advertising firm where I was working. By the age of twenty-two, I had approximately thirty-five papers around the country carrying my "Rock USA" column. Shelton Ivany, the editor of *Hit Parader* at the time, saw my column and asked me to write some stories for them. In less than a year I had taken over *Hit Parader* magazine."

Andy has turned his *Hit Parader* connection into a string of magazines, a record label (Titanium Records), various TV shows, including *Heavy Metal Heroes* and *Heavy Metal Hot Shots,* radio programs, telephone 900 numbers, catalogs—anything he can think of. Andy succeeds by looking ahead, seeing the big picture: "I look at the music industry as a giant wheel, and *Hit Parader* serves as the hub of that wheel."

The secret to expanding in the music business is this: Never let your job limit you. It should expand your horizons. You should use your position as a foundation for other projects that you'd like to work on.

## Parlaying an Opportunity

"The music business has gotten very competitive, and there are less labels," observes Dave Yeskel, vice president of sales for the Windham Hill group of labels.

Since opportunity can come in very odd situations, you need to be sharp, be on it, and be nice to everybody. You can't force things, but when an opening is available, move with the strategy of a football play—when there's a hole in the front line, see it and go through it quickly. You've got to jump when the opportunity's there. If you get tackled, you get up and try to run again. Don't give up. You're bound to encounter frustration as you move up the career ladder. That's just part of the business game.

Keep your eyes open. There's no way to predict every opportunity that's going to come along. Explore different paths. If you're with a record company, look at other companies. If you're in the media, look at additional outlets. An opportunity is anything that will tie in with the field you're familiar with, that will allow you to expand your realm of influence and your financial returns.

"When Atlantic Records did a deal with Mammoth Records, I got offered the position of the director of publicity at Mammoth, which is in Chapel Hill, North Carolina," recalls Jill Mango. "It was really scary and difficult to move down from New York to Chapel Hill, but I was ready to move up to that next level—director of publicity—so I took advantage of the opportunity."

Seeing and making the most of an opportunity depends on your personality. Everybody encounters opportunities every day. You tend to remember the few great ones that you missed, and the few great ones that you grabbed. But look beyond your great successes and abysmal failures. It's a matter of seeing them, not seizing them.

Here's another sports analogy: If you have a hundred pitches to swing at, you have a better chance of hitting the ball than you would if you were only allowed one swing. The more you see (that is, the more swings you take) the better your chances of success.

You need to see the pitch coming if you're going to take a swing. How do you develop that skill? Good question. It's just got to click. A lot of it is a matter of innate sense. You hear somebody say something and you see the vision—a moment of business clarity.

> **Commit it to memory:** *To move ahead, you need to see a concept, expand on it, and make it beneficial for yourself without doing harm to anyone else.*

Brainstorm the idea until it grows into something that can build and grow. Labels see these opportunities all the time. They have grabbed artists, force-fed them to the public, and made them stars. It's happened with bands like the Knack, Milli Vanilli, Bon Jovi, Guns N' Roses, Nirvana,

Stone Temple Pilots, the Spice Girls, and the Backstreet Boys. Bands are always being formulated, packaged, and sold. Shouldn't you do the same thing with yourself?

# Bon Jovi—Wanting It Bad

By the time he was a teenager in Sayreville, New Jersey, Jon Bongiovi was convinced that one day he would be a rock star. It was the 1970s, and the area's local music scene was rocking with rising stars like Bruce Springsteen and Southside Johnny and the Asbury Jukes.

"That was so close to my backyard," recalls Jon. "When you're thirteen, fourteen, or fifteen years old, you can't help but hear about it and have it affect you. When you went down to Asbury Park, what was once the crummy boardwalk became Americana. What was splintered wood became sacred ground, and you went, 'Ooh, aah.' And those things romanticized the idea. The myth became the legend, and one thing led to another, and I think blind faith is what got me here."

By the time he was sixteen, Jon was playing clubs. The club owners would make him sit by the exit, just in case the police came and started checking IDs. Out on the scene, Jon hooked up with keyboardist David Bryan, who played with him in a ten-piece rhythm and blues band called Atlantic City Expressway. Jon also performed with bands called the Rest, the Lechers, and John Bongiovi and the Wild Ones.

Wanting to get ahead, Jon got a job in 1980 from his second cousin, Tony Bongiovi, cleaning the Power Station Recording Studio. At the studio, he recorded a demo of the song "Runaway." That song came out on the radio in New Jersey, and soon it became something of a cult hit. A local radio station included "Runaway" on a compilation tape, and then the song started getting some serious airplay. Jon wanted to capitalize on his success by touring the New York clubs to support the single. He hired guys he knew from gigging on the Jersey shore. First, Jon gave Dave a call, who, in turn, tapped Alec John Such and Tico Torres. Richie Sambora signed on, and the band came together. They began gigging around New York in earnest.

The group opened for the band Scandal in New York and caught the attention of record exec Derek Shulman, who signed them to PolyGram. Their self-titled debut album came out on January 21, 1984.

Over the years Bon Jovi has sold more than 75 million albums. In addition to being a big solo artist in Europe, Jon acts and models clothes for Versace.

"I did my first record when I was twenty or twenty-one. I've grown up in public," says Jon. "The good thing is, I have a lot of great experiences; but the bad thing is, people see your baby pictures for as long as you live."

# Cliché #1: Who You Know

Luck is part of success, no doubt about it. This kind of luck can be described as, *Who you know at the right place and the right time.*

"I went to a Christmas party at IRS records in their SoHo office. I really loved a lot of their music," recalls Jill Mango. "As it happened, IRS had a position open to do college radio promotion. It was at a time before Nirvana and alternative, when college radio was still in this really interesting state. The woman who had done college radio was starting to focus on alternative radio, and she needed someone part-time. I was still in school, so I did that. Then the whole Nirvana explosion happened and everyone started pouring money into college radio. It was an interesting turn of events to experience."

# Mentors

Mentors are a beautiful thing. A mentor is someone who will hold your hand as you conquer the great big music business. Some people have one mentor; others have many. You can seek the help of a mentor at any stage of your career. Maintain the connections you already have and keep making contacts with people you respect and admire. One day, the guidance only these people can provide may make all the difference.

"I get the biggest kick out of backing intelligent, hardworking people and watching them succeed," notes Doug Morris, chairman and CEO of the Universal Music Group. "As you get older, it's a joke if you think you're going to go into some club and sit there with a bunch of young kids and be able to understand what music is great and what isn't. That's just ego talking. You need people who live and breathe it to help you. And your job is to pass on to them what you've learned over the years. I think of the record business like a sports team."

A mentor is a key person who's usually a bit older than you. He's been in the business longer than you have and he knows the ropes. You may have worked on different projects together, and he knows your strengths. He'll give you career guidance, and let you know of opportunities that may appeal to you. The best way to capture the interest of and develop relationships with mentors is by being good at what you do.

"Mentors are pretty important," confirms Jill. "Mine are always looking out for me and recommending me for jobs."

It's a very good idea to stay in contact with and in the good graces of former colleagues and bosses. A guy you worked with at a management firm on a band like the Gigolo Ants may become the vice president of product development at Warner Bros. Records. You share a past and a mutual passion for a project. Those are good bonding elements. If you are easy to work with, your enthusiasm will reward you down the line.

# Finding a Mentor

These days, Ted Cohen is executive vice president of Digital Music Network, Inc., but once upon a time he was a junior working at his college radio station. He was a terrific guy and someone said, "Oh, I'd like to work with you."

"The first guy who gave me my break was named Lynn Doyle. I told Lynn I was not going back to school senior year and was going to try and find a job. He said, 'Would you like to work with me? I'm the buyer of a chain of record stores.'"

Ted's first job in the music business was as the buyer for thirty-four stores.

"I met a lot of people really quickly because, at the time, a buyer for a thirty-four–store chain was considered a buyer for a major record chain. I'd get calls from Warner Bros., from Atlantic, from MCA, from all these different labels. They'd say, 'We want to meet with you about ordering.' It was a nice break.

"I became friends with the people at the Columbia Records office in Cleveland. They said, 'You should be doing promotion. We're going to get you a job.'

"I didn't realize until a few years later how nice it was that somebody mentored me, took me under their wing and said, 'We're going to give you a job.' I went to Cincinnati. I was the local guy for Columbia Records for a year. Thirty people had applied for the job. I was told, 'Go down to Cincinnati. You're going to interview with this guy and he's going to hire you. The interview is a formality, but you've got the job.'

"I thought that was the way it was: People helped you along. Once I figured it out, I got into helping other people along."

# Power Attitude

> ***Commit it to memory:*** *Success is all about never giving up, while at the same time not being obnoxious and overbearing.*

If you're going to succeed, you need to have the right attitude. Success is all about balance and keeping a positive attitude. Even if someone doesn't return your phone call the first few times, call back each week and leave a positive message.

You're going to find that many of the obstacles that are keeping you from expanding your career come from you. The best way to overcome these obstacles is to be optimistic and continue to want to learn.

"Knowledge is such a powerful thing," observes Marilyn Williams, account manager at Ad Personnel, a headhunting service in Los Angeles. "You can overcome most obstacles as long as you're prepared to listen and learn. It's basic and simple advice that's very difficult for some people to follow. You've got to push the obstacles aside and continue to want to learn."

## Cliché #2: Right Place, Right Time

As good as it is to be in the right place at the right time, being in the wrong place at the right time really sucks. This is going to happen a lot if you live outside the music scene. If at all possible, live where there's some activity in your line of work. If you've gotten as far as you can in the local music scene, perhaps now is the time to consider that big move. There are music hubs all over the country—Orlando, Seattle, Atlanta, Chapel Hill. Give yourself the opportunity to be great in the music biz by living close enough to someplace where it's happening.

Once you're in the middle of it all, moderation is the key. The music business offers many distractions—there's always a party, a concert, a dinner, or a band you can hang out with. Sometimes you'll make the scene for fun, other times for business. If you're trying to get somewhere with your career, the ugliest word in the English language is *busy*. Lots of times people will say they're busy when they're doing a lot of nothing. The people who really accomplish things are people who work with a lot of focus and get a lot done. Those are the people you should respect, admire, and network with.

The number one objective for anyone striving for success is to maintain focus on the task at hand. Nothing or no one should get in the way, whether it's where you are or who you're with. Once a task is done, move it aside and move on to the next one, keeping your career objectives in sight at all times.

## Start Early

If you're reading this book because you're considering the music business, and you haven't yet taken the plunge, here's a word of advice: Start early. Many people begin working toward this goal in their teens, because that's where their passions lie. If you're into music, and you're playing it, taking pictures of people who play it, putting up posters for your friends' bands— whatever—this counts as experience. Experience is a beautiful thing to have. If you're praying that someday someone will pay money for your services, get some credits on your résumé. Start small, start local, and build from there.

*Sage advice:* An easy way to advance your career is to start local and build.

## Passion

Another characteristic that will facilitate your career rise is passion. Love what you're doing, and you'll go a lot further.

"You definitely have to have passion about what you're doing," confirms Jill Mango. "In this business, passion will get you at least a part of the way."

What turns you on? What is it about the music business that still gets you excited? Or, if you find that your tastes or your lifestyle have changed as your career and your knowledge have grown, what is it that gets you excited today? When you're looking to change positions, you have to be visible, be out there, show people that you love what you're doing and would be a tremendous asset to their team. Be a huge music fan. That's why you got into the business in the first place, right?

## Make Friends

People enjoy working with people they like. Make friends with those in your department, on your floor. If your career has longevity, you will keep meeting the same people time and time again. If they like you, they'll want to work with you. You never know where someone is going to be five years from now.

"Where do I want to be in five years? That's a good question," admits Jill. "I really like the independent world. I like Wind-Up Records, the level of label that I'm at. I enjoy taking the bands to the interviews myself, and doing stuff like that. I don't see myself being the VP of publicity at a major label and having a huge department under me. I like the hands-on feeling of being in touch with the music."

## The Right Job for Your Personality

Some people create a position for themselves. Others take what they're given. Depends who you are. Do you have leadership qualities, or do you prefer to be told what to do? Do you have a vision, or are you better at executing assigned tasks? Take stock of your personality and decide what's best for you.

"I like working with other people, so I wanted to work with a record label," declares Jill Mango. "Because I was such a fan of the Mammoth Records roster, I'd been in touch with the publicist down there quite a bit. When she decided to leave, she immediately thought of me because I knew the artists."

If you choose the other route, and you're creating a job for yourself, make sure you've got some security before you start. You didn't learn how to swim by jumping into the deep end. You started in the shallow water and once you mastered the basics of swimming, you went to where you couldn't stand. In business, it's the same. Get the hang of working for yourself before you're ready to drop your steady income and head into the potentially treacherous waters of self-employment.

"I created a career for myself," notes Andy Secher. "I liked the music industry because it was fun. I didn't know where it would lead. I was working in advertising when I began in the music field, and I didn't expect it to be a full-time career. Then I realized I was making more money from my music column working two hours a week than I was in advertising working forty hours a week. It seemed too good to be true, but I didn't want to put all my eggs in one basket. I was working two different jobs. I had the security of working nine to five but was trying to create my own career. Once I saw my own thing working, I left the real world and started focusing on my career."

## Choosing Your Specialty

Choosing what area you will specialize in is a matter of skill and practicality. A lot of people just starting out would like to continue in the area in which they majored in college, but that doesn't always happen, and wasn't necessarily meant to be.

Where you start out or where you go to next may not be where you stay. Jill Mango is responsible for most media coverage on all the artists on the Wind-Up Records label. She began as a journalism major, interning at magazines. A job in the publicity department at *Rolling Stone* and a part-time stint in the editorial department at *Spin* gave Jill a chance to see both the publicity and the editorial side of things. She decided that she preferred being in publicity—pitching music ideas to the media.

Jill circulated. She interviewed and met people. Through networking, Jill landed an assistant's job in publicity at Atlantic Records. Low on the corporate ladder, she had what was considered the rather undesirable job of dealing with all the incoming phone calls. But she parlayed that into some great contacts, getting to know all the writers by taking their messages. She also made up all the guest lists for press parties, so she got to know everyone by sight when she checked their name against their face at the door.

**Remember:** *It's always good to look familiar.*

## Are You Willing to Move?

Once you've got your foot in the door, and you've paid your dues in the music industry hubs of New York and Los Angeles, you may want to consider the advantages of moving outside the big cities. In this era of independent distribution and independent labels, there are a lot of opportunities out there, and a little experience can go a long way.

Don't know where to start? Look in the classified section of *Billboard* magazine or, if you're the wired type (which is a skill you really need to succeed in the music business), check out *www.insiderz.com*. This Web site bills itself as "The ALL ACCESS PASS for professional members of the music and entertainment industry to network, share information, gossip, take cheap shots, and generally let it all hang out."

Click on the "Get Gigs" section and you'll find a variety of job opportunities—from a record distribution company looking for a sales representative in upstate New York to a director of media relations job in Minneapolis.

Once you're in the loop, it's easy to get promoted by moving around. If you're willing to work with the smaller companies, advancement and credential building come quickly.

# STAIRWAY TO HEAVEN:

## *Movin' on Up*

> I have ins to companies, so when I'm speaking to people I can assess where it is they want to be. I have to get into their heads and figure out, "What is it that you want to do? What is it that would be of interest to you?"
>
> —MARILYN WILLIAMS, HEADHUNTER, AD PERSONNEL

## Jobs That Are Right for You

Your ultimate goal might be a job in A&R (Artist and Repertoire), signing bands to record deals. You can wait and wait and wait for someone to offer you that position, and you may never get it. On the other hand, there are plenty of positions you can excel in on the way to reaching your goals. You can find a position that's interesting and challenging and work your way up the ladder.

"I didn't have a clue about what I wanted to do," notes Kathy Acquaviva, former major label publicist who is now CEO of the public relations firm Kathy Acquaviva Media. "I worked for an incredible gentleman at the Starwood nightclub, and I was perfectly happy. Then I was offered an opportunity to go to a record label. But I was happy at the Starwood. My boss at the club said, 'You have to take this job. It's a great opportunity and you can't refuse it.'"

Getting the ideal job is like finding a great relationship: People who wait for the perfect match often end up (a) disappointed and (b) very unfulfilled. Work is that way, too. Get out there and do something similar to what you want to do. Then keep your eyes and your mind open to opportunities. Peter Mench, the manager of artists like Metallica, Madonna, Hole, Smashing Pumpkins, and AC/DC, started out in the mailroom at a record label. He wanted to be in the music business and would do whatever he could to get there. Now he's one of the most respected managers in the business.

Nothing in life is set in stone. You get something that works for your personality, you grow into the job, and the job grows with you. Sure, you have to know your own skills, but you adapt, too.

"I've become a better writer over the years," confesses Andy Secher. "I don't know if I was a skilled writer in the beginning."

Don't wait for your dreams to come true. Take what you can get and make it work for you.

If you're lucky, you have an employment opportunity that gives you room for lateral growth, that allows you to experiment and grow with it. Don't wait for the ideal scenario: When you find a career move that interests you, jump in and see if you fit. ·

> **Commit it to memory:** *You've got to take what comes along and play with it a bit. If it doesn't work, get out. But you can't just sit around waiting for the ideal opportunity, or you're going to end up with big holes in your résumé.*

## Assessing Your Skills

If you have a good skill set, whatever that skill set happens to be, there are people looking for you. Can you be objective about where your skills lie? You have to if you're going to be hired for a specific position. Anyone hiring you wants to figure out who you are and where you fit in. So do you know where your strengths lie?

"It's human nature: People always see themselves as good at their jobs," Marilyn points out. "You ask anybody if they're good at what they do and invariably they'll say 'yes'—whether it's true or not."

People who know their skills usually have a relatively clear understanding of their path. They envision their future. They realize their skill set. They recognize where they want to be. They know whether or not they want to manage people. Some will say they want to be in distribution—they love putting product on the shelf. Others will say they enjoy marketing and promoting an artist. Whatever it is you want to do in the music business, you've got to understand what skills you possess and how you can use them to get from where you are to where you want to be.

Here are some basic things you should know about yourself when you are preparing to move up the ladder:

- Who you are and what you want
- Who you work for and what you do there
- Where you see yourself in the future as far as opportunities within your company
- Who supervises you and who, if anyone, you supervise
- Where you worked previously and why you left
- What your role was in your last company
- Whether you've worked as an independent contractor
- Whether you've worked individually
- Whether you've worked in a team environment
- Whether you can work in both individual and team environments
- What computer skills you have
- Whether you have a designer's eye
- Whether you can write well
- Whether you are good at "selling" ideas to people

This information is important in assessing whether you are a leader or a follower.

"Over the years, if you don't get too compartmentalized, you can pick up a pretty varied skill set which has implications outside your niche," notes Ted Cohen of DMN (Digital Music Network). "You could work in the promotion department, but still have appreciation for a good publicity campaign, which can lead you into special promotions, which can get you involved in radio . . ."

# Corporate Versus Independent

Before you make the final leap into a position you want, make sure you've considered whether you prefer working in a corporate environment or in a small, independent one. There are advantages and disadvantages to both.

## *Corporate*

Do you like daily interaction with a lot of people? Do you enjoy walking down the hall and going out to lunch with friends? How about brainstorming, and stopping by a colleague's office to ask, "What do you think of this?" Do you like meetings where there are a dozen people kicking ideas around? If your answer is yes, then a larger office environment is the one for you.

"Brainstorming is a beautiful thing," notes Dave Yeskel, vice president of sales for the Windham Hill group of labels. "Some things completely lend themselves to obvious ideas, other times it gets very creative: You just start thinking about new ways of doing things. Here's this record, what's the message, who's it being aimed toward? A good team allows you to go above and beyond where you can go on your own."

Working with an expansive music company—and that could be label, management, booking, distribution, whatever—will allow you to pick up a lot more components to your skill set than if you were working in just one area, especially if you are in an assistant's capacity. At a label, you may learn marketing, product development, promotion—all sorts of things. When you take a position, it's like declaring your major. Are you going to get a job in marketing, product development, or business development? Options abound until you choose or are chosen for your area of specialty.

As they get older, many people in the business move into the corporate side of things. The nice thing about aging in the music business is that you've gleaned a lot of knowledge coming up the ranks. The more you know, the better. Knowledge is power, so you just move on up, not with just one person, but with many people. That's what makes so many good companies function—people with a lot of talent and years behind them, so they understand situations. They've seen all of the cyclical happenings in music and in business, so they're prepared for it.

There's a lot to fathom in the business side of the music business, and if you're still wet behind the ears, you probably haven't grasped that much yet, or worked on a large variety of projects. You will find that the knowledge you glean from years of accrued experience can help you do your job better.

But moving up the corporate ladder always requires discipline. Once you've settled into a position at a large record company, you'll be working at least 10:00 A.M. to 6:00 P.M., fifty weeks a year, doing pretty much the same tasks, over and over.

## Independent

"I'm not one to be told what to do," states Andy Secher. "My attitude is that most people are basically incompetent, so I'd rather do it on my own, and be totally responsible for a project's success or failure."

Creating a job—like being a free agent—isn't for everyone, particularly if you're not self-motivated. You know yourself. You know what works best for you.

If you like the ability to move around and take a Thursday to yourself, and you want to stay in the realm of liberal arts, you should think seriously about self-employment. That way, your work depends solely on what you create. You can do a little bit of everything for everybody.

"At any given time, I've got half a dozen clients, and the job description of what I'm doing for one is totally different than what I'm doing for the other five," explains Ted Cohen. "You basically have to be able to apply what you know to the situation and do a needs analysis of what the client wants and expects from you."

The millennium transition finds us at a time when there is less and less job security. A growing number of people are leaving the corporate womb and going the self-employment route. As the corporate world downsizes, there are many opportunities for people to work as independent publicists, independent marketing consultants, independent sales agents—the list goes on and on. Independent status gives you the opportunity to manage different projects for different companies and different artists; thus, you end up cross-pollinating your relationships.

"I get to make the decisions now," asserts Kathy Acquaviva, who launched her own independent publicity firm after overseeing publicity departments at Atlantic, Hollywood, RCA, and Virgin. "Instead of a team of people, it's basically myself who decides who I want to represent, which type of music I want to handle, if I want to move from music to other areas. Whereas working on the corporate level of a record company, your path is pretty much laid before you."

If you can mold and shape the direction of your business and your career, you're very lucky. If you're stuck in one of those positions where what you have to do is cast in stone, then you have to make the most of more limited possibilities.

## Headhunters

In addition to mentors and contacts, headhunters offer you another way to advance in your career. Headhunters are contracted by employers to fill specialized positions, and may be looking for someone with the very skills that you possess. Oftentimes, the people they seek are already employed, and are willing to be lured away by a more enticing offer.

A good headhunter is a beautiful thing because she will work with you every step of the way. She will prepare you for every interview, negotiate your salary—she'll do whatever it takes, as long as she believes you're a worthy candidate. Headhunters have to work with people they believe are going to get a job offer; otherwise, they don't get their commission.

"My job is speaking to people, listening to them, and then finding them a position that they really want," maintains Marilyn Williams, account manager at Ad Personnel Headhunters in Los Angeles.

A headhunter can only work with the skills that you've got. If you're supervising the printing of CD covers for Capitol Records, then you could probably get a job with PLG Printing, but your headhunter is probably not going to be able to set you up with a job at Top Rock Management.

"I can only represent people who have a strong background and want to stay in that arena," confirms Marilyn Williams. "The company who's hiring is not going to pay me a fee to bring somebody to the table under a scenario that he's good at this, but he wants to do something else. We have to be very realistic with our candidates and tell them up front, 'If you want to change your career, we can't help you. But if you're good at what you do and want to stay in your career, we can definitely help you.'"

Look at your desirability. Think about the university you attended: Harvard, Yale, and Stanford always look good. But other universities impress as well. A writer coming from the Walter Cronkite School of Journalism at Arizona State University carries a lot of clout; so does a broadcast journalism or business major from New York University.

Next thing a headhunter will look at is where you've worked in the past. A little time in corporate is always good. A stint with Warner Bros., Sony Music, Capitol, EMI, BMG, Universal—any of the major players in the industry—gives the headhunter some insight into how well you work within a fixed structure.

Corporate has a very strict set of rules. Your headhunter, who will undoubtedly attempt to place you in a corporate position, will tell you that business maturity weighs very heavily in determining where you'll be hired.

"Experience matters a lot. I look on their résumé," confirms Marilyn. "If someone has already worked at Atlantic Records, they've already got a track record. I need to look at people's track records. When I get a résumé coming across my desk, I have to look at that résumé, and see what jumps out at me. If there's nothing on the résumé that jumps out at me, I'm not inclined to talk to them. It's a waste of all our time because I can't represent them."

Whatever headhunter you go to will first determine your credentials. Once she's established who you are, she'll attempt to assess your character because she wants to know how you work best. Can you lead a group or do you work best independently? Are you a decision maker, or one that executes and implements?

"My job is to get into their heads and figure out, 'What is it that they want to do?'" offers Marilyn. "If I'm assessing them and they tell me something that is not relevant to what I can do for them, I tell them right there and then, 'You know, John Doe, there's nothing I can do for you.' However, if everything they tell me is positive, and it sets off bells in my head, I think, 'Yeah, I'm able to fit you into wherever.'"

Certain career inclinations quickly come to light. If you think outside the box, an independent situation may be better for you. The indies

are far more open to wild marketing ideas and novel distribution concepts. Corporate jobs are all about working with others and not stealing anybody's thunder while you make a name for yourself. They're more about being a member of a team and having a fat expense account.

One important thing to keep in mind when changing positions is that how you view your qualifications is not nearly as important as how the person who's going to hire you views your skills.

Your headhunter will ask you questions like, "How would you record a hit album?" And then she will wait and watch what your reaction is.

"They may laugh. That's a good indication to me," says Marilyn. "Hey, yeah, weird question, but how do you answer it seriously? It depends on the individual personality, but it also depends on whether you can think outside the box. It doesn't matter what you're designing, you've got to go about the steps the same way."

Your headhunter will want you to answer the question step by step so she can see what your thought process would be. *This album is supposed to make you money. If it is supposed to make you money, who do you go and talk to in order to find out what kind of album to make?* You talk to the people who buy albums. *What is the consensus of opinion? What is missing from the marketplace? What needs to change? What do you need to do to make this more accessible so that people are going to buy it?* You need to talk to your clients or your customers, and then you have to go about designing the music to fill the public need. *How are we going to do this? What are you going to have the band play?* When you're selling the album, you need to go and talk to the marketing department and find out what promotional ideas they have come up with recently. What budget and time constraints do they have to work with?

"If I ask a question, and they go, 'What the . . . ?' and can't answer the question, I will give them help and hints," adds Marilyn. "Sometimes people catch on. Others are like, 'Duhhh, forget it.'"

Your headhunter may quiz you with a completely irrelevant question, such as **Q:** Why is a manhole cover round? **A:** The manhole cover, which is a little bigger than the manhole, won't fall through the manhole if it's round.

That's the answer, but it's not the only thing that your interrogator wants to elicit from you with that question. He wants you to think about it, show how you use logic. If you are one of those really brainy mathematical types, maybe you'll think of the manhole cover in terms of physics and spout off some complex concept. That's cool. Your interrogator just wants to know that you're thinking something beside the fact that this is a stupid question. He wants to determine how you think for yourself.

## Job Happiness

If you find a job that suits your skills and lets you grow, you should be happy, because then you can make it into what you want. Look for possibilities involving lateral and upward growth so you can grow with your work. And by all means, if an area in the industry interests you and seems like it would be a refreshing change from what you're doing now, give some serious consideration to going for it.

> ***Commit it to memory:*** *Set goals, and use your career moves to reach them.*

"When I prepare candidates for an interview, I always ask them where they would like to be in five years, because that's a question interviewers like to ask. I suggest they answer the question like this: 'I want to continue to learn and grow,'" advises Marilyn. "The reality is, none of us know what we can truly achieve in five years. As long as we're prepared to continue to learn, we're on the right track."

Life is all about learning and growing. Since work is a big part of life, your work should be mind-expanding, and help you see possibilities for branching out. You'll be doing one thing, then all of a sudden the lights will come on and you'll be someone else. If you leave the gates open for what's to come, then you will probably be looking back five years from now and saying, "Wow! Look what I've achieved!"

# CAREER DECISIONS:
## *Creating Your Own*
## *Opportunities*

> Nobody would sign the Police. That's how I started my record
> business. I just thought, "I hate somebody telling me no."
> —MILES COPELAND, CEO
> ARK 21 RECORDS

*T*here have been contractions and expansions in the music industry for years. With the merger of MCA and PolyGram to become
Universal Music in 1999, and the subsequent mergers of EMI
and Time Warner and BMG and Sony, what were once the big six
record companies—PolyGram, WEA, Sony Music, BMG, EMI, and
MCA—are now three—Time Warner, Universal, and BMG. Employees
and bands at major labels are getting laid off by the hundreds.
Independent labels—be they Interscope, Epitaph, Righteous Babe, Wind-
Up, or the like—are on the rise. Distribution channels are in flux because
of the Internet and MP3 compression systems, which allow the listener to
download near–CD-quality songs in a matter of minutes. It's an exciting
time, and a great time to advance your career—if you know how.

## Out on Your Own
Ted Cohen, executive vice president of Digital Music Network, Inc.,
worked at Warner Bros. from 1971 to 1984, then went right to Westwood
One radio syndication. In June 1985, he found himself out of work for the
first time in his life. He'd been in a corporate womb for fourteen years.

"There was this stigma—Is anyone going to call me back? Is anyone going to agree to see me?" Ted wondered. "I discovered, (a) if you're good at what you do, and (b) if you try to be relatively a good person, people will take your call whether you're working or not. People will pay attention to you whether you're at a big company or operating out of your home office."

Cultivating relationships requires staying in touch with people. As with all relationships, finding the proper balance is key. Stay in touch, but don't be a pain in the butt.

"I always joked that whatever my shortcomings are, they're equal opportunity," laughs Ted. "I'm more inclined to call somebody back when they're out of work than to call them back if they're working. If they're working, they're not that insecure. If they're not working, that callback means a lot more."

Your attitude toward your business colleagues has a lot to do with creating opportunities for yourself. It's been said by motivational speakers from Anthony Robbins to Dale Carnegie: You should be the type of person other people want to be around. Then people will want to work with you no matter what.

## Be Creative

In the realm of self-employment, to get what you want you've got to be persistent yet positive. Oftentimes, it takes months to get your potential clients to sign on the dotted line. For example, maybe the guy who was recruited to run the emusic Web site is not sure if the site is 100 percent effective from a client and marketing point of view. In September, the two of you started talking about his retaining you to refine the Web site. You talk weekly, you shmooze him and nurture the relationship, and in November you ask, "Now?"

And he says, "No, not yet."

In December it's still "No, not yet."

You call him in January. "Now?"

He says, "Look, I really want to do it. Send me a proposal."

So you send him a proposal stating what you would do and how you would improve the site, without giving away all of your tricks.

Your contact is encouraged. "Fine. It looks great, it's just not the time. I'll call you Monday."

Monday comes . . . Monday goes . . . Tuesday comes . . . Tuesday goes. You start to write him an e-mail, something along the lines of: *You promised you'd get back to me, it's now Wednesday* . . . WAIT! Think! You want the business. You have no option but to be nice. Instead of lacing into him, be creative, send him a powerful e-mail, uniquely styled. You could write it as a personal ad saying something along the following lines:

*POSITION WANTED: Dynamic Web consultant seeks online music site to make history with.*

Be positive: treat him like a potential partner, not a potential enemy. You may be surprised by the response. Perhaps he sends back an e-mail saying, *Gee whiz. I think you're cute. You want to go out next Wednesday, say three o'clock? Please confirm.*

He liked it. You meet Wednesday at 3:00 P.M. and at 3:15 you're hired. Had you written him the *You've let me down again* e-mail, you might have gotten back a response along the lines of, *Well, let me* really *let you down.*

**Commit it to memory:** *When looking for work or recruiting new clients, always be positive and creative. A good idea presented in an upbeat fashion goes a long way.*

We're in a business where we're supposed to be creative. Sure, the music is important, but you can probably find five records with similar production values or similar music aesthetics, and one is successful; the other four are not. What makes one band a hit over another group is the marketing and how the record is positioned. Your personal success will depend on the same approach.

# The Right Attitude

Once upon a time, a gentleman by the name of Les Brown really wanted to work as a disc jockey. So every day he went into a radio station in Philadelphia and said, "I want to work here. Are there any openings?"

And every day they said, "There are no openings. Come back tomorrow."

Without fail, the next day Les would return to the radio station. Sometimes he'd bring in fruit or flowers for the receptionist. He was always smiling and upbeat, although he was constantly getting rejected. Still, he kept at it.

Those around the radio station admired his perseverance.

Finally, one day he came into the radio station, and the program director asked, "Can you go on the air right away? The deejay's sick."

That was his big break. Les shone and became the morning voice on that station for ten years.

He went in with the positive attitude of, *I want to work here,* but he wasn't obnoxious or overbearing about it. He played the game according to the rules set by the radio station, and it paid off.

Playing by the rules of your hopefully future employer is extremely important. If someone says she needs time to make a decision and she'll get back to you in a week, wait a week and a day before you call her. If you harass her into making a decision before she's ready, inevitably that answer will be *no*.

## Creating a Job for Yourself

Deciding to go out on your own is a difficult decision. In corporate, everything is handed to you, from the paper clips on the desk to the artist you'll be working with. You may have a great boss who asks, "Who do you want to work with?" And each staff member may be able to choose, "Well, I like this band, and I like this band." That way, the team can work with artists they really love, and the artist will get the most out of their development.

When you head out on your own, it's all up to you. Nobody's giving you office space with a desk and a computer. There's no medical insurance. Those elements all have to be handled by you.

So is what you're going to do. Do you remember people asking, "What do you want to be when you grow up?" Well, now you're grown up and you can be anything you want that people will pay money for.

You can also choose any area of specialty. What kind of music do you really like to work with? Which artists would it be a pleasure to represent? Do you want to sell their albums? Go out on tour with them? Play with their money? Promote them? It's your gig. Choose wisely. Start small and grow.

Hopefully, you'll get to a point in your business when you can't say *yes* to everything offered you. For some offers that come your way, you can't think of money; you have to think of what you really like. As an independent, you may find that you don't want to take on a client you don't really care for. Could you really, seriously enjoy being a roadie for Air Supply?

"I did record company publicity for twenty-two years," observes Kathy Acquaviva. "When I went out on my own, I realized I could publicize different types of things; I didn't have to stick with music. I moved into other areas—film soundtracks and an author named Andrew Vox who writes suspense novels. The promotion I did was for his eleventh book, which was about blues artists. Relativity Records put together a CD of those blues artists. That was a great project—totally different for me."

## You Can Do It All

One of the great joys of self-employment is that you can wear many hats and do so many cool things that you're never broke or bored. Ted Cohen's sideline consulting business, Consulting Adults, offers a database of different talent that Ted hires according to each project.

"On one project I may work on it myself, on another project I may have three people involved," says Ted. "On another project, I may bring two people in who aren't working on the third project. The job goes to the best people for the task."

Say there's a project for Universal Studios. Consulting Adults may bring in two people to work on the project. When the Universal project is finished, each of those people gets a check and happily goes their own separate ways.

In the era of corporate downsizing, voice mail, e-mail, and virtual offices, doing work on a project-by-project basis is a great way to avoid becoming overstaffed, understaffed, or creating an overhead situation that isn't manageable from project to project.

> ### A word to the wise consultant: *Avoid the tendency of walking into a situation and saying, "What you ought to be doing is . . ." They hired you because there's something specific they needed done. Always keep your core function in mind.*

If you build up a roster of a half-dozen companies, you've got a good business. And a good variety of businesses. Wouldn't it be cool if your client list included MP3.com, DreamWorks Records, the Hollywood Stock Exchange, Tower Records Online, Interactive Agency, and WebTV? Perhaps you're doing content acquisition for WebTV, new business development for Interactive Agency, label relations for Hollywood Records, and general technology evangelism for MP3.com.

Those would be exciting days. Your morning might include sitting with an artist and manager talking about why they should put their music up on the Web using MP3 audio compression, then working out a branding and technology strategy for the Tower Records Web site. In the afternoon you're putting together an event with the Hollywood Stock Exchange at the House of Blues for the Academy Awards.

"On one call we're booking a band. On another call we're deciding what the Web site is going to look like. Then I'm setting up the download to the Julian Lennon album on a broad band server," elaborates Ted about a day in the life of a successful consultant.

The great thing about multitasking clients is that your meetings become multitiered. You may take a meeting with Hannah Management to talk about getting the band Symposium to play at the Hollywood Stock

Exchange show, but you might also talk about the band committing songs for an MP3 download and doing a performance and interview for WebTV and Tower Records Online.

"I've been able to develop a level of trust in my clients," asserts Ted. "Yes, we joke that I might have four or five hats on at any given time, but everybody's getting a pretty fair shake."

As a free agent, you can usually develop a creative empire that is more along the lines of your dream career than if you held a 9-to-5 position. Just make sure that the stuff you do is synergistic, not parasitic. When you're working with clients, let them work together. Miracles could happen if you arranged for DreamWorks to work with MP3 on a campaign that the Interactive Agency is helping to enhance.

> **Commit it to memory:** *When multitasking, you have to be careful that your clients are not in competition with each other. If someone doesn't think you have his best interest at heart, then he's going to find someone he believes will do him right.*

# NETWORKING:
## *Doin' the Business* 𝄇

Networking is incredibly important. There is a level of powerful people in the music business who are definitely music fans. To connect with them in their environment and talk about music with them is really invaluable.

—JILL MANGO, DIRECTOR OF PUBLICITY
WIND-UP RECORDS

## The Key to It All

Just about the best thing you can do to advance your career is to network. You meet people, tell them what you're about, what you're looking for, and they'll say, "Oh, you should talk to a friend of mine . . ." In a perfect world you've got a lead into a great new career path.

"I have to go out and socialize, that's part of the business," confirms Kathy Acquaviva. "Ninety-nine percent of my time is spent covering concerts, so you meet people constantly. You mix, you see people you haven't seen, you bump into people. It also tells people, 'Oh, that's right. You're doing entertainment.'"

Will Smith was known as the "Fresh Prince of Bel Air" when he met DJ Jazzy Jeff at a party and launched his Grammy Award–winning music career.

"I was already a rapper and Jeff was a DJ," confirms Will. "Jeff said that he was the best DJ in Philadelphia. He played at all the parties. He'd heard of me, but he already had somebody that he worked with. But then

Jeff played a party on my mom's block and I asked if I could sit in. Jeff agreed, and we played together. The chemistry between us was really great. So Jeff got my number and we got together."

Now, Will Smith is one of the biggest rappers in the world with tunes like "Gettin' Jiggy With It" and "Wild Wild West" topping the charts in many nations.

"For anybody wanting to get into the business, you've got to think about networking," advises Bob Chiappardi, president and CEO of Concrete Marketing. "Networking is the most important thing out there. I've got people working for me now who are making close to six figures. They started working for me as interns making $10 a day. If you want to be in the music business, you have to do a lot of stuff for free—or almost for free—at first. You need to be in the circles. You need to know people."

## Cultivating Your Contacts

The music business is all about who you can get to take your phone call, and who you know. If a manager you know calls you up and says, "I've just signed this great hip-hop artist, and I want you to help me promote them," you think, "Great, my network got me an opportunity."

Multiplatinum rock artist Rob Zombie got to working with producer Scott Humphrey on the *Hellbilly Deluxe* album because of an introduction.

"Scott fell into it in a weird sort of way," confirms Rob. "He was sharing a house with another producer, Charlie Clouser. I was working with Charlie. Both Charlie and Scott had a studio in the house, and, when Charlie left [to work on Nine Inch Nails], he recommended Scott. I didn't know Scott, but I started working with him just to see how it would go, and it went really well. It just happened because I met him through Charlie."

A friend of a friend or associate is a great way to meet new contacts, because you come with an automatic reference. No one is going to introduce you to anybody if she thinks you're a dim-witted dork. If you're well liked, you can end up with a lot of interesting work situations because people will call up and say, "We have a mutual friend who suggested that we get together and talk."

"The first time I went to South by Southwest was a huge break. I made leaps and strides as far as contacts," says Jill Mango. "I was introduced to a lot of writers and got into this certain scene, and it really translated when I got back to New York. I had tons of contacts through people I had met down there, so that was a real big bonus business-wise."

**Commit it to memory:** *Meeting someone by introduction is one of the most effective ways to cultivate business contacts because it gives you a reference.*

Once you meet these people, follow up. A phone call or an e-mail with a joke goes a long way.

# The Power of Positivity

Keep in mind a few key concepts when communicating with others. Since music is considered an art form, it is subject to opinion. No one is an authority on what is horrible, mediocre, good, or great. We all have a right to our own view, and we each deserve respect.

"No one likes a know-it-all. Few people like being negatively criticized. Most people do not wish to be patronized or hustled. Kissing up is not a winning method of communication," affirms manager Phil Frazier. "There is a difference between schmoozing, socializing, and using people. Most people in this business are aware of the value of contacts, savvy to the fact that others are trying to be successful in their various endeavors and wish assistance. Asking someone straight out what you wish from them is usually the best approach."

Wherever you are, whether it be at a party, at work, or on the bus, it is important to be proactive in creating an environment that is conducive to mutual respect and open-mindedness. That way, others will be more willing to listen to your wants and needs. "Create the experience of everyone having a good time. And then just spin," advises David Javelosa, composer, producer, and technology evangelist for Yamaha game developer relations. You're selling yourself; make sure you've got a product people want to buy, then get out there and do it.

"Buying somebody a drink goes a long way," notes Bob Chiappardi. "You have to be likable. The more personable and chatty you are, the more people like being around you, and the more likely they are to give you a position. It comes down to real basic needs—you need to project integrity and a willingness to work hard. Once you get that across, people will be apt to share their knowledge, help you learn, and present you with opportunities."

If you have a positive attitude, a spirit of sharing, without keeping score or expecting compensation, the activity of networking can be a highly rewarding and joyous experience. Even if you're not having a great day, project a positive image—compliment somebody on his dress, eyes, hair. Be someone that people want to have around.

"We like people who are particularly charismatic or particularly helpful—people who are making things happen," notes Bob. "Once you get a reputation for being reliable, people start trusting you to do things. You get to be like a pusher: The first taste is for free, then if you like it, you've got to pay for it. As your value and your stock rise, you can garner a better paycheck and more rewards."

## Knowing the People You Need to Meet

If you're pitching yourself for a particular position in a particular business, it's important to know who you want to meet. It's always good to know the head of the company, because a good word from her will go a long way. Who knows—you may be at a cocktail function and someone will say, "There's Gary Gersh." And you're thinking, He's the head of >EN entertainment network. I like where his company's going. I'd like to talk to him.

"If you don't know the inner workings of a company, you can invariably go into the wrong part of the business, which is a waste of time," asserts headhunter Marilyn Williams. "You've got to know the players. It's important to build relationships within the company and let these people know who you are, and what you do, and that you do a good job."

### *Sage advice:* Always be nice to secretaries!

A secretary knows more about the business life of the person you are trying to reach than anyone else. Making her an ally can give you access to valuable information. What's the best time of day to catch Mr. Big in his office? What's his travel schedule like? Also, you never know where that secretary is going to be ten years from now.

## The Back Door to the Introduction

Unless you're particularly cunning and aggressive, you don't consciously go out and say, "How can I meet the president of such-and-such a company?" Generally, you meet important people by backdooring the situation. You'll meet somebody and you have a good interaction. Then you'll get a phone call about one project or another. You meet with someone and work on a project. The president is interested in the project and you meet.

But you have to understand the ebbs and flows of each specific business to know how to best backdoor a situation.

By putting a solid amount of time into being out there and networking, you'll make people see you, and they will realize that you're in the middle of things, that you're in the loop. You never know who's going to show up at that TJ Martell Foundation Reception, the Herring on Hollywood symposium, or who will be backstage at that Ozzy Osbourne gig in Salt Lake City.

"A lot of musicians know about us and our records," notes Joey Peters, drummer for Warner Bros. recording act Grant Lee Buffalo. "We have developed some friends in high places, so we've been able to tour with the Smashing Pumpkins and Pearl Jam and R.E.M. In the case with Pearl Jam, they just happened to hear our record and liked us. They called us up and we toured with them for a month. With R.E.M. it was a case where friends of ours knew them and sent them our record. Vocalist Michael Stipe became a fan, and he was very vocal about it."

A friend of a friend of a friend of a friend—or a complete coincidence. You never know when a good business contact is going to come along.

Ted Cohen got a consulting gig with the Hollywood Stock Exchange by going to visit a friend's wife at the Mondrian Hotel. Their kids were playing out by the pool, while the parents chatted. Ted happened to be wearing a Prodigy Internet baseball cap. A gentleman came up to them and said, "Oh, do you work for Prodigy? My name is Doug. We're working with the Hollywood Stock Exchange. We should talk sometime."

## The Beauty of Business Cards

Business cards are absolutely a must. Everywhere you go you'll find somebody who will be interested in taking your card because everybody exchanges cards. It's standard business practice. You just never know when opportunity will knock. And when it does, make a positive impression. Be pleasant, make people smile, hand them a business card. It's protocol and, at the very least, it's a prop to make them think you're important. You'll know you're traveling in the right circles if every time you go to an event, somebody asks you for a card.

An effective business card should include the following:

- Your name
- Your business name
- Your phone number
- Your address
- Your e-mail address
- Your fax number
- Information on what your company does, if you choose

## Take Time

Your business contact is probably not going to offer you a job right off the bat. Usually it takes time to cultivate a healthy business relationship. Take a long courtship and get to know each other. If she's a good business contact, you may be working with her for years to come.

"R.E.M.'s Michael Stipe first became a fan of Grant Lee Buffalo in '93," Joey Peters points out. "In '95 R.E.M. asked us to go on the road with them."

Learn to read your associates, give them space to make a decision—and never force their hand. If you have your preliminary meeting and decide to stay in touch, call every week or so, or correspond by e-mail. Never get impatient, because you can't make someone commit to something until he's ready. It may take someone two or three months of getting to know you before he'll say, "This is someone I want to work with on a daily basis."

Don't push it. If he says he'll talk to you in a week, wait. If you press someone for an answer, you may not get the answer you want. Once, I was sitting in the office of Peter, a well-respected manager. He was thinking about signing on a British hip-hop act. As we were in our meeting, the act called. Peter picked up the phone and said, "Look, I told you I'd talk to you in a week. I told you I'd get back to you. You've now called three times in three days—so now here's the new thing: Don't call anymore. If the phone rings and I call you, answer it. Otherwise, do not ever dial my number again." And he hung up.

When asked what that was all about, Peter replied, "I explained to this group a week ago that I needed some time to make a decision, and they obviously didn't want to give me the time, so he got the decision. The decision was *no*."

> **Commit it to memory:** You cannot force people to work with you—they have to want to work with you.

## Reach Out and Touch Someone with E-mail

E-mail is an effective way of keeping your name on someone's mind. A joke, a pleasant thought, an idea—anything to show that you'll be a real asset to his team. Plus, when your e-mail gets on somebody's desktop computer, you get the eyeball factor. Your name stays on his mind. When he reads through his e-mails, yours will be there, and hopefully, he'll get back to you.

"I'm continually surprised when I will send an e-mail to somebody I don't have a daily relationship with, saying, 'Hi! Wanted to give you a buzz. Didn't know what your schedule was like. When's a good time to talk . . . ?' and I get an e-mail back saying, 'Call me tomorrow morning about nine. It sounds good,'" relates Ted Cohen.

If you have a detailed message, e-mail is a great way to lay out your case and at least get an answer back.

For bands, the Internet provides a direct means of contacting audiences and keeping in touch. "E-mail and the Internet are two of the most important business tools in marketing and developing a relationship with the audience," concludes Dave Mustaine, founder of the hard rock band Megadeth. "It lets them know that you are there and that you care for them. All anybody wants is to be needed and included. Keep them in the loop and they'll always be loyal to you. It's a great way to network with your constituency when you have time constraints."

# Section ii

## Career Paths: Where It's At

# BUSINESS OPTIONS:
## *Mr. Pinstripe Suit*

The record industry needs to become a more fascinating place
so that we can inspire talented kids to become musicians and
excite smart young executives to join the business and shake
things up.

—JIMMY IOVINE, COFOUNDER
INTERSCOPE RECORDS

## The Really Lucky Ones

*M*any people in the music business make a lot of transitions.
The key is finding out what you want to do. Some people—the lucky ones—just have their path laid out for
them. As soon as they start out, they're on their way. This
has happened for bands like Creed and Godsmack, as well as businesspeople. Take Michael Rosenblatt, the senior vice president of A&R at MCA
Records. He got into the music business when he was nineteen.

"I got a job working for Seymour Stein at Sire Records, so I moved
from L.A. to New York," Michael recalls. "The job was as a messenger boy.
But I knew that A&R was what I wanted to do, so I just started going out
to all the clubs, and I discovered a band called the B-52s. I had just turned
twenty when that happened. I'm over forty now and I've never been without a job."

Michael's job is to sell bands he thinks are worth signing to record
companies, because the record companies are the ones who will sell the
bands to the world.

"I don't call radio stations, I don't call Wal-Mart, I don't call *The Tonight Show*—I don't do that," notes Michael. "But all those people at the record company do, so I've got to get them very excited about the artist."

In A&R, the main question you have to ask yourself is, How can I get my team excited about this project? By getting them involved, by playing them the demos. Share the unmastered songs. Introduce the staff to the artists—especially if you have someone who's just a star, who just radiates it. Introduce your act to some of the key people in the company; they, in turn, will start working it around the building.

## Joining the Company

Not everyone has their career path laid out for them that easily. If you're like the majority of people in the music business, a career is something you'll have to build yourself, brick by brick. One way to do this is to work for a large company—such as a record label, radio station, management firm, concert promotion conglomerate, or distribution house—and work your way up the ladder. By working in a good collaborative environment, you'll pick up a variety of skills and knowledge beyond just the area you're working in. If you're looking to broaden your knowledge of the business process, working in a larger, corporate environment is definitely a fine choice.

People who excel in corporate are very dedicated to their company and their jobs. They incorporate into their business regime the necessary flattery and "brownnosing" that corporate life requires, and enjoy the perks—free travel, hefty expense accounts, free concerts and CDs, cool parties. Not a bad life—especially when your salary rises into the six-figure realm.

"I've never been one to want to start my own company," admits Hanna Bolte, senior director of media relations, West Coast, for BMI. "BMI is fine, and you get to learn a lot. There's never a dull moment. You never are working on the same thing over and over again. Everything changes, and it's good. And for me it's all about knowledge and what I can learn and what I can do and what challenges impart themselves."

If you're not working for a large corporation, you may experience frustrations that the employees of megacompanies avoid. One of the problems when working at a smaller company is that you don't have the clout of the Big Boys; there's nobody high above you who can make that power phone call to ABC, SFX, or Fox and say, "No, you have to put Creed on the Billboard Music Awards."

However, like everything else in this business, if you are dedicated and you keep working at it, you'll score. Suppose the independent label that employs you wants you to get this great band onto *David Letterman*. It may take you two years, but when you finally do succeed, you will have scored a major career coup. A time slot on *Letterman*—three minutes and thirty seconds—is extremely valuable. If you had to buy that as advertising time, it would break the bank, easily.

## A Shining Example

Bryn Bridenthal has soared in the traditional business environment— Elektra, Capitol, Geffen—and now as national director of publicity at DreamWorks. Music mogul David Geffen takes Bryn with him wherever he goes. She's well liked and well respected and has closely guided the careers of bands like Queen, Mötley Crüe, Guns N' Roses, and Nirvana. When asked how she could survive and thrive in a corporate environment, she offered this response:

"By being very direct, and as honest as humanly possible. It saves a whole lot of time and if you're telling the truth you don't have to remember the story. I'm so in people's faces and so pragmatic about it that people don't lumber me with a lot of bullshit. That way I can bat it out of the ballpark as quickly as possible."

A veteran of many music business situations—both private and corporate—Bryn has done it all, both as an independent, and now within the realm of a corporation.

"I always wanted to be independent because I thought that if I'm putting in 300 percent of my energy, I want the energy that I'm putting in to determine the compensation. When you work in a corporation you work in a structured salary situation. I thought it would be much better to be on my own and determine my own income," Bryn reveals. "When you're independent, you have to do your finance stuff and your tax stuff and you have to bill people. For me it was just a waste of energy. It's completely illogical, because you're not in control at a record company, but I felt out of control as an independent, and I'm a control freak.

"I really wanted to be on the artist's team, not the record company's team. What I found when I started as an independent was that I felt castrated by the artist signing the check. Somehow or other it skewed the relationship and I felt like I had no power whatsoever, and I felt like I was really corrupted and compromised and had to do the bidding. I just was completely uncomfortable with it. I found out I'm not an entrepreneurial personality, I'm a salaried-employee type of girl. I want you to hire me, pay me a salary, give me health insurance and take care of that aspect of my life so I never have to think about it again, so I can spend all of my energy in the actual process of the job.

"Corporate works better for me," she concludes. "Your whole livelihood does not rise and fall on any one artist. If you're an independent it does—if you're out on your own, your whole career can be at the mercy of one band. When I was out on my own, I didn't like that kind of pressure, which is why I went back into corporate. I like being part of the team. I have pride. I feel really good when I say, 'I work at DreamWorks,' because I have such admiration for the company and the philosophy and the people who are managing it.

"I also really love being in on the ground floor and building something."

## Your Role at a Record Label

The philosophy of the record label is: If we perceive that a band is going to make money, we will spend the money. Each player at a record label—whether it's the production supervisor, the national director of publicity, or the regional head of distribution—is part of a team that backs the band and works toward the common goal of making the band a success.

"Basically, our job is to take the vision of an artist and bring it to the consumer," observes Abbey Konowitch, executive vice president at MCA Records. "What that means in reality is you've got to get it on the radio. If you make a video, you have to make the right video that captures the right image for the artist. Then you get that video exposed in some way. You work with creative services so they can visually present your record to the marketplace. You come up with sales campaigns, and retail campaigns, and advertising, and the look of the point-of-purchase displays, and you have to make all of that work for the consumer. It's not easy. It's not easy on a lot of levels."

Playing both the artist side and the record company side requires a delicate touch, since, by nature, the relationship between the artist and the businessperson is an adversarial one. Is a record successful because the artist is brilliant? Is a record unsuccessful because the record company sucks? Obviously, there's a different window of opportunity with each act. A record company has to find that window and expand it—as long as the process is facilitated by the musician.

The difference between one band being successful and another band being successful is much more than the music, their album cover, or which tour they got on. It's the word that's spread about a band that makes it a success. Yes, the music is important, but you can play five records and they will all have the same production values and musical aesthetics because there's so much derivative music out there on the market. What makes one band a hit over another group is marketing—the cleverness of how it's spun out and positioned.

**Commit it to memory:** *In addition to the music, what makes an act a hit is the team behind it and the cooperation of the artist.*

# Getting Hired

Know your potential employer. In the weeks leading up to your job interview, do Web searches on your company, act like you're in the loop. It behooves you to understand what makes the business tick and why; then you understand the mechanics of it all. Figure out why record companies, publishers, and others in the music business make the moves they do—regarding staff, growth, cutbacks, which records they pick up, which ones they don't. Understanding these key elements of the business gives you a better idea of what makes this business tick. If you really want a career in any business, you'd better understand what fuels it, and where the money's really coming from, because at the end of the day that's what matters. The bottom line is this: Companies need to make money. The more you understand about where the money comes from, the better off you'll be.

A company is not going to hire you if you want to reinvent the existing model. When going for a job, maintain a positive attitude, just as you would if you were working for yourself and trying to solicit clients. Use the attitude of "Yeah, we can do this," as opposed to, "This will never work."

To get hired, you need to show a good understanding of the music.

"I really understand the music I work with and I really like it, and I try to work with people who share that same passion," notes Marco Barbieri, vice president and general manager of Century Media Records, a hard rock record label. "If they're experienced, that always helps. Most of the key players in the company are people I've worked with before or other people have worked with before. They have experience working in stores or being in bands or fanzines—stuff like that. Those are tangible qualifications that help people to do the job. I want someone who's honest, someone I can get along with, and someone who has the same personality that the rest of the staff and I have, because working together you become a really close-knit group."

# Pinstripe Blues

"It was extremely tough making the transition into corporate," notes Vince Castellucci, senior director of licensing with the Harry Fox Agency. "It's a feeling of a loss of freedom."

When you're a musician playing on the road, you usually get to control who you play with, and the only time frame you have to deal with is when you have to be onstage, or when you have to make a bus or airplane or when you have to be in the studio. In corporate, it's 7:00 A.M. to 10:00 or 11:00 P.M., every day. The higher up you go, the more time you have to put into it.

"I like to think that it's very well worth it," admits Vince. "I love music. And if you don't support the artists, they can't afford their art; their integrity—that music—will erode the intellectual establishment. The artists, musicians, and writers won't be able to support themselves and they'll find another job. Then you'll have schlock music out there and the real talent will find another way to support themselves and their families. By staying in corporate, I'm trying my darndest to keep my habit of listening to great music going by making sure that the music is properly licensed and that those royalties are paid and they're fulfilled."

Some people do great in corporate, while others are truly uncomfortable and not suited for the traditional working environment.

"I like the word 'suited,'" chuckles Mark S. Chasan, composer/arranger and founder of emusic.com. "When you try on a suit, it either fits or it doesn't. If it feels and looks good, you're 'well suited,' especially if it provides you with an air of elegance and power. If it feels awkward, annoying, restrictive, too baggy, too heavy, it either needs altering or you just don't wear it. But what is corporate structure? Corporations are run by people, and just as people are different, so are corporations and their structures. So if the corporate structure isn't fitting or working, either tailor it or try on a new corporation."

In any business scenario, balance is the key. Be in control, be out of control, share control—whatever your balance may be.

"Relating it to music, the bottom line is that you have to make a move to get ahead," notes Mark. "Sometimes that move involves giving up control and trusting others, even if they are record executives."

# *Your Own Business*

Sony, WEA, Universal, EMI, and the notorious BMG. They can always give Chuck D a call, and I can tell them exactly what to do with the Wild, Wild West. I can give them a template. But it will cost each one of them royally.
—CHUCK D, PUBLIC ENEMY
DIGITAL DOWNLOADING ENTREPRENEUR

## Brave New World

"Change is inevitable, and everything is about to change," says Chuck D, the rapper who leads Public Enemy, and one of the first groups to venture into the world of online sales and music marketing.

The music biz is ripe and ready for conquering. It started out with the rise of the independent label in the early nineties. Now that the number of multinational conglomerates has been cut in half, there's a more level playing field. The major labels now resemble major league baseball teams, and the independent labels are like farm teams: They nurture their players along until they've sold 20,000 units, then the majors swoop in for a hit-and-run deal.

"The majors are not much into artist development or selling to niche markets because the expenses are too high. They have to go in for the big kill," notes entertainment industry attorney Owen Sloane.

In other words, the marketplace is wide open for finding and developing bands and making a good career for yourself in the music biz.

## The Geek Shall Inherit the Earth

Something most people over thirty-five do not understand is the power of the Internet as an alternative medium. Because of the Internet and quality audio streaming, the music industry is reinventing itself. Suddenly MP3 technology allowing audio downloading and streaming puts the entire music universe on your desktop. Music is becoming a cottage industry, with more people getting small chunks of the big pie. It's a beautiful thing. Big business is no longer able to rule. It's anybody's game.

"The Web is the biggest revolution to hit the music business since the advent of recorded sound," notes Al Teller, founder of AtomicPop.com and former chairman/CEO of MCA Records.

When Jimmy Iovine, cofounder of Interscope Records, was asked where he thought the music industry was going, he offered the following answer, "It will be some sort of indie—fill in the blank, I don't know. But it's going to be an indie, it's not going to be the majors, I'm telling you. It's going to be Gary Gersh [former president of Capitol], or DreamWorks, or somebody we don't know yet."

There's a new business model out there. Perhaps you can take advantage of it.

> **Commit it to memory:** The Internet is changing the music business in ways we can only imagine.

## The New Business Paradigm

Because of the coming of age of the Internet, we will soon have a global music industry with no borders, where record labels can manufacture and supply and distribute in one place, and sell anywhere in the world without having to go through different countries, different hands, different distributors.

"New technology in present-day contracts is an oxymoron. Your contract holds your butt back," Chuck D said when severing his contract with Def Jam Records to handle his own marketing and distribution. "Technology is leveling the playing field. No longer can executives, accountants, and lawyers dictate the flow. MP3 won't destroy the record companies. It just will split the market. The Net opens the way for artistry and entrepreneurs."

## Creating Your Own Business

Let's say you want to start your own record label. You're probably not going to be able to compete with the meganational conglomerates like Warner Bros., Universal, and BMG. You'd need millions of dollars of capital plus access to one of their distribution networks. Unless you're really smart, well connected, and lucky—like Mo Ostin or Jimmy Iovine—you're probably not going to get there. But, for a marginal investment, you can create an exciting and profitable record label that's run by a group of friends and keeps all of you busy and gainfully employed.

"If we didn't have a record deal, I would explore manufacturing the records ourselves," says David Lowery, formerly of Camper Van Beethoven and now in Cracker on Virgin Records. "I'd make an arrangement with an independent distributor, maybe hire some Internet marketing firms, make deals with MP3 sites, and run the business more like a software company. I would like to see if doing it that way was going to afford us more creative control and make us more money and get our music to the people we think would like us."

What kind of investment do you need to start a label? You should have no less than $50,000 in the business bank account—preferably $100,000—though it's possible to start with as little as $5,000 (prepare for a diet of peanut butter sandwiches.)

"I've been accused of being a dreamer, I've always had lofty goals, but I've made most of my goals materialize," notes Marco Barbieri. "I'm always setting game plans and goals for myself and for the company. I have a lot of interest in a lot of different things that I want to do, and I try and incorporate that into my job. I see myself as an entrepreneur, trying to accomplish something."

Creating your own record label means finding good bands, a recording studio, an engineer, a producer, and a distributor. It also means investing your money or searching for somebody else who believes in your band's music. It means long hours, sleepless nights, and sketchy profits.

"Initially, I got outright loans with a payback percentage rate and started that way," explains Tom Viscount, lead singer and the primary writer for Viscount, and founder of Lost Coast Records. "People came to my shows. They heard the gigs. They liked what I did, and we were in business together. I had about $20,000–$25,000 given to me for recording costs to get the CD done."

Tom had been an actor and done voice-over work prior to recording *My Name Is Nobody,* so he had a reputation. Familiarity is always a good thing. It makes people remember you and subsequently sells music.

It's really hard to start a record label with a band nobody's ever heard of, as Iara Lee knows well. She's a filmmaker and music-label entrepreneur in New York City who has produced more than a score of CDs, with more to come, including a series of CDs featuring music inspired by works of architecture.

"I'm not swimming in profits," admits Iara, "but success should be monitored not just by profit, but by the cultural relevance and impact that you have."

# Specialization

Having a label that specializes in a specific kind of music is both a good thing and a bad thing. It's good in that you develop a reputation, and you're marketing the aura of the label as much as that of the band.

"I wanted my Zombie A Go-Go label to be specific so that you could be a fan of the label," declares Interscope recording artist Rob Zombie, founder of Zombie A Go-Go Records. "You wouldn't even have to know what the band was; you could just see that it was on the label and know that you would like it."

Zombie A Go-Go Records releases albums by bands like the Bomboras and the Ghastly Ones, and compilations like *Halloween Hootenanny*—weird monster surf rock music.

As long as you stay within markets of your genre, it's pretty easy to promote bands on a specialized label. Once you try and expand a band's fan base beyond your established boundaries, it may be difficult, but those obstacles can still be overcome.

"There's a far greater benefit in specializing in one kind of music—like at Century Media, we specialize in heavy metal," notes Marco Barbieri. "You know the market, you know the audience. We like to think that we know what's good and what people want to hear, and we specialize in it. If you try to diversify, you usually wind up screwing up because you're trying to take a piece of an existing market someone else already knows much more about and has the best bands. You have to remember what your foundation and your roots are. That's what our fan base wants."

# A Label's Essential Ingredient

The first order of business has nothing to do with business: You need music. Taylor Clyne can't even play the triangle, so when opportunity knocked, he opened the door. In 1996, Taylor was in an agent-training program at William Morris when two college buddies of his brother's had an idea worth investing some time, money, and effort in. The idea was an album of punk rock musicians singing old TV theme songs.

Taylor left the agent-training program and he and his brother, Andrew, forked over about $35,000 to create Which? Records and produce the CD *Show & Tell: A Stormy Remembrance of TV Theme Songs.* Apparently at least one of the *Diff'rent Strokes* cast members was out on parole, because Todd Bridges and the Whatcha Talkin' 'Bout Willis Experience became *Show & Tell*'s premier band.

Taylor and Andrew's friends, Scott Pollack and Jake Szufnarowski, logged in a lot of the man-hours marketing the product. They became the merchandising and marketing departments. They had a good understanding of the music and were able to get the word out. In 1997, Which? Records had sales of $80,000.

## It's All About the Artist

There are three things musicians want from a major label: money for recording and touring, national marketing muscle, and wide distribution. Most artists have also said they would rather sell 200,000 copies of ten records each than 7 million of two. Artists prefer staying power; they want the label to nurture their careers.

"When a band signs to a major, they give them about a month to do something," Rob Zombie points out. "If they don't explode, they're history. You never hear from them again. You've got to give a band time to do something, to develop into something. Which no one does anymore—everyone's just looking for that hit of the moment. No one's trying to develop a career."

Developing an artist takes a lot of time. To begin with, you have to make sure that you're on the same page, career-wise, so folks at the label need to educate their artists. Artists need to know how their contracts read and what it all means. You may have to explain how the album has to recoup the investment, or what a mechanical account is. If you're going to run a successful independent label, you have to make sure the artists know this stuff; otherwise, later on you may have differences of opinion and misunderstandings.

If you're going to sign a band, you should believe in them and do a bit of research into their background. Make sure they're a good group of guys who have their heads on straight. You also have to make sure that they understand what they're getting into by signing that contract. So many bands think that once they're signed, their work ends and the label does everything for them. Not true. It's definitely a team effort: The label motivates the band, the band kicks the label in the ass—now that's a good partnership.

> **Commit it to memory:** *To make any band business partnership work, you have to listen to each other.*

You need to listen to each other. Where does the band want advertising to be placed? These are basic points, but they need to be covered. After taking into account the band's wishes, the label needs to create a marketing plan and to think, Okay, what do we want shipped out on street date? What do we expect the first week's sound scans to be versus the first quarter? Versus the first year? Then, working together, you go after it.

Hopefully, you'll achieve your goals. Sometimes you won't reach all your goals in the first quarter; sometimes you'll exceed your own expectations. But you just go with it, and push forward.

How you work each band varies. Not every band deserves to be a priority on its first release—you realize it is a first record, it is what it is, and depending on the band (each band is different), you work to create something. Much of what you do to create a buzz is formulaic, but you also do things that relate to just this one band, and you hope that people catch on. If it doesn't happen on the first record, then hopefully the band is good enough and they'll create a better work—and work it better next time around. You just keep doing it until it breaks. And even if everything is perfect, it still doesn't mean that you're going to have a successful band, but you've got to give it your very best shot.

## . . . And the Numbers

The music business requires long hours, but those who are in it are dedicated. "You'll work your butt off," promises Brian Herb, founder of Mother of All Music Records. "It takes a strange kind of person to get yourself into this industry. Most people aren't doing it because they want to make a million dollars. They're doing it because it's something they have to do."

And the numbers aren't too bad, either. To make money off album sales, it's merely a function of numbers. Which? Records sells CDs to its distributor, Caroline, for $6 each. Caroline adds $4 when it sells the CDs to the retailer, and the retailer adds $2 to arrive at the retail price of the CD. If you've sold 27,614 CDs at $12 apiece, receiving $6 per CD, you're making some serious bucks—$165,684 to be exact. Just remember: You don't actually receive the $6 from your distributor until *after* your CD sells.

## Reasons *Not* to Work with a Band

Should you ever choose *not* to work with a band even if you love their music? Yeah. The music is very important, and you can have an excellent band, but if they don't have it together, that's going to have an impact on your relationship. It doesn't matter whether these problems are financial, personal or interpersonal, or relating to substance abuse. You're investing a lot of money in a band and you hope that someday it's going to pay off. If it's not right, it's not worth it. And while it sucks at the time, you have to think, Well, down the road, it really wouldn't have been so smooth.

Personality is a big factor. There's a lot more to the music business than just music and business.

## Being in Charge

Most people who create and manage start-up labels grew up living and breathing the music industry. It's all they've been interested in for the past twenty years. They don't leave the office at 6:00, they surround themselves with this stuff twenty-four hours a day, and they never burn out on it. Leaders are obsessive. They're motivated; they work morning to night.

"Being in charge of a label means I have to take care of everyone. I have to make sure that they stay focused, that they know what our priorities are, and that they have the materials in order to do their job," notes Marco Barbieri of Century Media. "I have a good staff of people, many of whom I took from other companies, or they have bands and did radio shows, did something like that so that there's some experience there. They're all big music fans, and that helps. Just to make sure we're all on the same page."

Smart label managers make sure all pertinent information is shared. Surveys of decision making in companies reveal that rapid and decisive decisions normally stem not from intuitive and extraordinary leadership but rather from an established and well-organized system with access to all the relevant data. When a team has all the information, they can quickly reach an informed decision.

"I like an open working environment," admits Marco. "At other places, the management is more closed-door: They tell you what to do, you don't have any input, you just do it, and that creates resentment. At Century Media, it's an open environment. Anyone can say anything to me and anything to the owners—they'll listen to it. This creates an environment that's really creative and fun to work in, and people feel like they're involved."

Marco, who runs Century Media for two European owners, basically has free reign and is the point person for all of North and South America. He's heavily involved in the promotion and touring. He deals with a lot of bands on a day-to-day basis on the road, making sure that they have what they need, that they know where to go and what to do.

"I don't like to think of myself as management. I'm not a coach on the sidelines," Marco contends. "I like to think of myself as more like a captain of a football team, that I'm out on the field with everyone. I don't have any special office, I don't need anything special, I want to be with the guys in the trenches and work together. That way they can respect me, if I practice what I preach, and that way I can respect them better."

# Making Mistakes

You'd like to think that once you're on your way, you continuously make money. But dead record labels, like A&M, Geffen, Enigma, Def American, VeeJay, and DGC, will attest that that's not always the case. Life in the music business doesn't always work out peachy. In 1998, Which? Records had sales of only $26,000.

They had only one follow-up CD for *Show & Tell*, and when it tanked, Which? Records had no other bands to back it up. "We were too picky," admits label founder Taylor Clyne. "We really overlooked the fact that we should have been working on a steady stream of records." Meanwhile, based on misguided 1998 projections, they rented cushy offices in New York City. Compounding problems, their backup band, the Shining Path, didn't want to tour. "Make sure your band will go on the road to promote their record," Clyne insists. "A kid in Nebraska won't buy a record from a band from New York if they don't get to see and hear that band live." Which? Records sold fewer than 500 Shining Path CDs in the stores, another 2,600 on tour, and made $5,000 by selling a song from the album to a TV show.

Which? Records has since learned from its mistakes and projected $150,000 in sales in 1999, based on a line of CDs in the works, including a jazz band performing Grateful Dead songs.

# Managing People Well

The first step to becoming a really great manager is simply to use your common sense. Management is about pausing to ask yourself the right questions so that your common sense can provide the answers.

When you become a manager, you gain control over your own work; not all of it, but some of it. You can change things. You can do things differently. You actually have the authority to make a huge impact on the way in which your staff work. You can shape your own work environment.

The manager of a small team has three major roles to play:

## • Planner

A manager has to take a long-term view: The higher you rise, the further you will have to look. While a team member will be working toward known and established goals, the manager must look further ahead so that these goals are selected wisely. By thinking about the eventual consequences of different plans, the manager selects the optimal plan for the team and implements it. By looking ahead, not only to the next project but to the project after that, the manager ensures that work is not repeated nor problems tackled too late, and that the necessary resources are allocated and arranged.

### • **Provider**

The manager has access to information and materials that the team needs. Oftentimes, he is the only one with the authority or influence to acquire particular things. This is a crucial aspect of the manager's role simply because no one else can do that job; there is some authority that the manager holds uniquely within the team, and he must exercise this authority to make the team work.

### · **Protector**

The team needs security. In any company, there are short-term distractions that can sidetrack the workforce from the important issues. The manager should guard against these to protect the team. If your team is undertaking a new project, you are responsible for spec-ing it out (especially in terms of time), so your team is not given an impossible deadline. If someone on your team comes up with a good plan, you must ensure that it receives a fair hearing and that your team knows and understands the outcome. If someone on your team has a problem at work, you have to deal with it.

# Virtual Staff

These days, everything can be virtual, including your staff.

Doing business in the new millennium is all about contracting. Think of it as building a building. If you were going to build a house, you'd start with a plan, a blueprint. Once you have your vision sketched out, you would hire people to build it—the mason, the carpenter, the electrician, the plumber. You would hire whichever skilled laborers you needed, as you needed them.

Using this model, your business becomes a loose aggregation of colleagues that you bring in on different projects. Instead of a staff, you call up friends who have computers and phones set up in their spare bedrooms. One project may involve one person, another project may require three people. On another project, you may have two people who aren't working on the third project. It all comes down to who the best people are for the task. When you're finished with the project, you go your separate ways.

Having a virtual staff keeps your overhead low—a beautiful thing.

In the era of corporate downsizing, voice mail and e-mail, and virtual offices, it's a great way not to find yourself overstaffed, understaffed, or creating an overhead situation that isn't manageable from project to project.

With your new virtual record/management/promotion/booking company, if you need an accountant for your taxes, you hire her in

February, well in advance of the April 15 deadline. You outsource the services you need instead of incurring astronomical costs on a consistent basis. If you keep things streamlined, hitting your bottom line is easy.

## Sharing Your Assets

After going out on her own and forming Acquaviva Media, Kathy Acquaviva wondered if anyone was going to call her. Would anyone see her? She found that reputation matters.

Becoming a specialist in one area has lots of advantages, as you can make material stretch to work for more than one client.

"I've had clients ask, 'When you walk into a certain company, are you presenting us, or are you presenting a bunch of people?'" recalls Ted Cohen of DMN Consulting. "If I were calling a certain company on behalf of a certain client, then it becomes my decision if I want to see him about that one act, or if I make the appointment saying, 'I've got a bunch of stuff that I want to talk about.' It's all about developing a level of trust in my clients."

By cultivating your relationships and staying in touch with people when they're working as well as when they're not, you keep your responsibilities balanced.

# SELLING ALBUMS:
## *Give It to Me Baby*

There is a tremendous amount of satisfaction to be had in taking a release that is drenched in the musicians' and the label's
blood, sweat, and tears and adding in our own to make it a
success.

—ALICIA ROSE, VICE PRESIDENT
NAIL DISTRIBUTION

## Move Music

Selling records requires a combined effort by the promotion and
distribution teams. More often than not, these are record company jobs that pay well and offer good bonuses for meeting and
exceeding quotas. Working in distribution also gives you a lot of
responsibility.

The distribution dude is responsible for getting all releases by his
record company into record stores, and any place else that will sell music
in his marketplace. The field of distribution—more so than many other
areas of the music business—requires a team effort.

"I have three regional salespeople who work for me and a distribution company that I work with," explains Dave Yeskel, vice president of
sales for the Windham Hill group of labels. "Distribution is all about
sales—talking to the accounts. It's developing relationships, it's presenting
a good product, it's having a strong marketing plan. It's having all the tools
you need to try and convince the retail outlets that you have a product that
can sell some records."

## Distribution Details

The distribution company is the field force that distributes records. These guys are the soldiers—they're the ones who are actually out in the field making sure that music gets to the masses. Generally, one distribution company will handle a conglomerate of labels. For example, BMG distributes music for Windham Hill, RCA, Arista, and several other labels.

Every distribution company has its own manufacturing plant where it prints the CD, assembles the package, shrink-wraps the product, and distributes it. The cost is about $1.70 per CD for the first thousand, then the price drops the more CDs you have pressed.

The major labels all have their own distribution companies; the smaller labels and artists use independent distributors. At the turn of the millennium, record distribution is in a transitional stage. Companies are being bought and sold and names are changing overnight.

> **Commit it to memory:** A distributor's goal is to help expose a given record or series of records to a broader audience.

## Buyers

Distributors are in touch with buyers on a daily or weekly basis. They're taking inventories, putting up posters, helping to set up promotions, planning lifestyle marketing, and delivering samplers and other kinds of cross-promotional tie-ins.

The distributors sell records to the buyers. Buyers are the people at the accounts who are responsible for purchasing the music at wholesale price, adding in their percentage, and then selling it at retail prices to the masses. There are many types of buyers—genre buyers, catalog buyers, new release buyers. Each chain of stores has a different modus operandi.

Take Tower Records, for example. There are about a hundred stores in the Tower chain, and each store operates completely independent of the others: Each makes its own buying decisions, has its own budgets, does everything on its own.

Musicland employs a contrary philosophy. With about a thousand stores, give or take a dozen, the Musicland chain purchases product for virtually all its stores from a central purchasing office—a handful of people make the decision about what goes into the stores on a local, regional, and national basis. Store autonomy is minimal. If a record does break out of Musicland's particular market and a store runs out of stock, the store can order it through the central office. The vast majority of music retail chains operate in this manner.

The buying power of individually owned, mom-and-pop stores differs according to the type of music. If you're selling alternative or rap, independent stores will account for a much larger percentage of your sales than if you're handling genres like jazz, New Age, and classical.

Different stores also sell to different demographics of music consumers. If you're distributing New Age or light jazz, stores like Borders, Barnes & Noble, Tower Records, Sam Goody, and Media Play will be good matches, because these stores tend to sell to an older age group.

## The Math of It All

There are documented facts and figures to help you determine how well a specific genre of music will sell in the overall marketplace. SoundScan is an information and data-sorting service that compiles all of the sales from every store in America. The actual calculation of the sales is done much like political exit polls, in which a number of stores in a certain market are examined to see how a particular record has performed in that market, based on the stores' percentages of business in the marketplace.

"Today, you know what's selling where. There's so much more calculated information available at our fingertips. We have a much better understanding of how and where and why records sell," explains Dave Yeskel.

Ask Dave and he'll give you the details of Windham Hill's position in the music marketplace. "My genre—New Age—counts for less than half a percentage point of business. That's everybody combined. Windham Hill accounts for 60 to 70 percent of that market. We are definitely the leaders in new age. We do very well with smooth jazz. We're starting to develop urban adult contemporary records."

A record label calculates how many units it can expect to sell of a record by using mathematical formulas. One of the aspects that figures into the calculation for sales is what the market will bear. There's also the issue of the artist's deal. The bigger the star, the more money is spent in an attempt to sell records. Another way a record label projects sales is by simple comparison: This artist reminds us of such-and-such a band—what did they sell?

Sales expectations tend to be low for new artists—unless you have a powerhouse marketing plan, or you know something's going to happen. For example, when Columbia released the first Mariah Carey record, she was a new artist. Sure, she had great songs and a sultry presence, but she was also married to her record label president, so there was obviously going to be a big push made on her record's behalf. Mariah Carey's debut album probably shipped close to a million units because they set it up so well. Usually, for a new artist playing a specialized genre of music, ten thousand copies will be distributed to key retail outlets.

"You can call it within five thousand pieces," notes Dave. "With established artists, you look at the history. You look at what they SoundScanned. You look at what they shipped out on the last record, what returns came back in. You figure the net out, and on the next record you put out 25 to 40 percent of the net of the last record. It's not as easy as A plus B equals C; it's like, if A equals X and B equals Y, then C will probably be Z."

Label executives make calculations, but they're not black and white by any stretch of the imagination. There's a lot of flexibility, because so many different factors have to be taken into consideration. The unpredictability of it all is what makes this business so beautiful.

Also, the industry is evolving. Distribution outlets are changing as buyers' computer systems are being brought up-to-date. Today, buyers know what they can sell—the information is there right in front of them on spreadsheets. Some outlets buy based on a mathematical formula, relying on very little personal input. If a record company's national objective is 100,000 units, and an account makes up 5 percent of the national average, then the distributor should be able to sell that account's 5,000 units.

"It's gotten a lot tighter . . . a lot more competitive . . . a lot more scientific . . . a lot more black and white . . . a lot less fun," observes Dave. "There's always been a tug-of-war between art and commerce, but commerce is winning."

Record sales have become lean and mean because record companies have become big business. Selling records is a means of manipulating the companies' stock prices. This has come about because of the rash of corporate takeovers that occurred in the music industry during the nineties. The business paradigm has shifted from looking to long-term profits to judging success and financial positioning on a month-to-month basis. This method of judging talent is far less forgiving than the old ways of artist development, when the biggest acts in the business took time to cultivate an audience. U2 took time; R.E.M. took time; Led Zeppelin took time. But these days, performance in the music business is tied to quarterly earnings reports.

"There is no doubt that the reporting of quarterly numbers is something that is counterproductive to the creative process," insists Jimmy Iovine. "People on Wall Street have got to come a little bit closer to the record business to fully understand it, so that they don't hurt the companies they are interested in investing in. When you try to jam an album out just to make the numbers, it damages the music. It damages careers. And while all that hocus-pocus might look good on paper in the short run, it will damage the company's future prospects in the long run, too. You don't ever hear about anyone at Coca-Cola calling up their managers and screaming, "Hurry up! Ship out more Coca-Cola! I don't care if you have enough time to put the right amount of sugar in it. We've got to make our numbers!"

Today the music business is all about a company's stock prices. Stockholders want to see profits, and they want to see them now. They don't want to see them five years from now; they want to see them *now*. This whole "now" concept is weighing heavily on the music industry.

This hardcore profit motive will change in time, especially if the companies are sold off. The record industry is a very fluid business, but at the moment these companies are no longer independently owned; they're part of huge conglomerates. Change would require a shift in the attitude of the parent corporations. Take Universal Records, which is run by Edgar Bronfman, Jr. If Universal's parent company, Seagram, said, "Don't worry about the stock price. Take all the time you need, take all the money you need, do what you need to do. It will all be a wash in the end," the music business would go back to the star-driven careers that supported it throughout the nineties.

The other alternative is for the labels to release a lot fewer records and market them right.

## Independent Distribution

When a band is just starting out, distribution is always a mess. Mark Mothersbaugh, cofounder of DEVO, recalls a time back before they had a record deal or a record contract. They were pressing 45s in DEVO's native state of Ohio. In the mid-seventies, it cost $400 to press one thousand.

"We did the graphics and we folded the covers, and put them together ourselves," recalls Mark. "I'd drive from Akron to Cleveland . . . and go into record stores and say, 'Hey, need some more DEVO records?' And the guy would say, 'Let me see.' He'd go down to the last aisle and look through a bin that was labeled something like 'Assorted,' and say something like, 'No, still got the one we got last week.' And that was our early independent record distribution network. We were doing that every day, whenever we could fit it in with our day jobs. I was a maintenance man at an apartment building so I had more free time than some of the other guys, but we were all doing that kind of stuff."

There are easier ways for artists to get their music out to the masses. Independent distributors are a very viable way to sell albums. Many of the independent distribution companies have developed their own specialized brand of record labels. The person who owns the distribution company has his own retinue of independent labels that do A&R. Essentially, the distributor is signing bands, and signing with any distributor is basically a positive step for an artist or a label. There are very few retailers that are loyal to any one purchasing source.

"The best way to find who is doing independent distribution is to go to a record store and ask who they buy their records from," says Kathy Callahan, senior director of western regional sales at Windham Hill Records. "It changes every year as to who's a player and who's not. There's a lot of consolidation on the independent side of music these days."

One very successful independent distribution company is NAIL Distribution. NAIL was founded in 1995 to fulfill a specific need: to effectively place Northwest independent music in Northwest stores. NAIL's initial family of fifty labels—primarily Northwest artists—has grown to over four hundred labels. NAIL is now proud to offer almost five thousand titles by Northwest (mainly Oregon and Washington) artists.

"We're regionally focused," affirms Alicia Rose, vice president, head buyer, general manager, slave driver, and queen for NAIL Distribution. "NAIL is a distributor for bands and labels that are regional (in the Northwest), that have an appeal and an audience in this region. In order for us to distribute an act, they have to have done a good job on their end: They have to go get press; they have to work on radio; they have to work on word of mouth; they have to tour; they have to do everything. All we're here to do is sell records."

NAIL has a far-reaching distribution chain that extends throughout the world. But, in truth, NAIL is what you would call a regionally focused national distributor with international exports. Most distributors don't focus on distributing material from one region, but the reason this company has survived is because it is regional.

NAIL's distribution process is simple. Let's say a band signs a nonexclusive distribution deal with NAIL. The distributor will take thirty CDs by faxing a purchase order to the label. Once NAIL has them in stock, it takes the one-sheet description and puts it on the NAIL news release fax that goes out every Friday.

NAIL doesn't charge for its services; instead, it works on a markup of the product. Some distributors work on a percentage, and some distributors work on markup. If a band says, "I want to sell you my CD for $7," that's the price on the sale of the CD that the band will receive. The distributor then marks up the price of the CD by whatever its percentage may be. Some distributors mark up at 16 percent, some distributors at 30 percent. Then they sell the CD to the record store for that price to get it to the masses.

Another significant music distributor is KOCH International USA, one of the leading independent distributors in the United States. The company boasts the largest marketing and sales department of any independent U.S. distributor, with seven regional sales offices and a marketing and sales staff of over forty music professionals. For financial reference, KOCH International was ranked number 315 on *Inc.* magazine's list of America's 500 fastest-growing private companies in 1991.

## Home Free

Once an artist gets a distribution deal going, he's home free. If the CD is going to a big chain store like Tower or K-Mart, it is sent to the company's regional distribution facility, where it is counted, inventoried, and sent off to the appropriate stores. The smaller companies get packages drop-shipped to them. It depends on the number of stores in the chain and the deal that's set up.

Sometimes CDs are sent to a one-stop. The name comes from the term "one-stop shopping"—when you used to be able to buy everything you needed for your record store in one place. A one-stop would sell accessories and whatever you needed to set up shop. These days, it's just a place where you can buy every CD available from every different label. The prices are generally a little higher than if you were buying directly from the manufacturer, but it's convenient nonetheless. A one-stop will sell to everybody; it sells to the independent store, to the chain store—to whoever has the credit.

## Expanding Your Reach

If you're thinking of becoming an independent distributor, there are two obvious ways to broaden the range of your exposure. One is mail order; the second is the Web.

Mail order is a great way to go if you have product that goes beyond the mainstream.

"We thought, okay, we've got independent distribution, but we're doing heavy metal, so there are a lot of stores that won't carry our stuff, even though there are a lot of kids who want it. That's why we tried mail order," explains Marco Barbieri of Century Media Records. "Building distribution is a slow process. You begin trying to promote the fact that you have mail order, whether it's stripping it into the records or inserting a catalog into the record. We insert a foldout so that you can see some of the title. The foldout also tells you more about the mail-order service and has advertisements."

Century Media's mail-order campaign is basic: It uses a common sense approach, and it didn't require the investment of a lot of time or money.

"We've been fortunate. We've gotten a great response to our stuff," notes Marco. "It continues to build a nice catalog."

Tie-in trade with other labels through strong marketing and promotion has helped Century Media build up a database of 40,000 kids in the United States. Online efforts support mail order. Century Media posts its catalog online so people can mail order from it.

Century Media's mail order has been doing so well that the company expanded to handle upstart bedroom labels by kids it reached through fanzines. The thought was to help them out. The project has been so successful that both domestic and European labels have offered to handle the mail order. It just snowballed to the point where Century Media is now representing a couple of thousand titles for other people. The company now has a 3,500-square-foot warehouse packed with different labels' materials.

"The assistant to our retail guy was calling stores just for promo tracking and making sure that people have the products in stock," notes Marco. "Then he started doing direct sales for other musicians who didn't have distribution here. He's turned that into his full-time job and someone else's full-time job. Now we've got what looks like a one-stop, with two guys selling import stuff and they're selling them to some three hundred different accounts, and it's great. It rivals the money that we make through our distributor in the U.S."

## Online Distribution

People still like to shop in record stores; they like to hold the product in their hand. But hip young record stores have started to cater to a new type of consumer who doesn't have to go into record stores, and doesn't necessarily want to. This new consumer is buying online.

Additionally, there is more music being made than there is shelf space in distribution outlets. Other avenues must be developed to sell product that is not readily available in the retail marketplace. If you're looking for a hard-to-find jazz record, the chances of it being in most mainstream stores is minimal. So you go online to a big distribution site like Amazon.com, you order the CD and get it in two or three days, and the whole process is much more pleasant than going from store to store in search of one CD. The simplicity of locating hard-to-find albums is what makes online distribution so appealing. It is a new and expanding method of distributing CDs.

"Online distribution is a big business," points out Marc Geiger, a principal in ARTISTdirect, a triple-faceted entertainment venture that includes the online music purchase site *www.UBL.com.* "It's not like CDs and record stores are going away, but you can generate $16 billion with no manufacturing or distribution costs—so, obviously, profitability goes way up. And when people are getting their music, you can serve them ads which create new revenue streams for the record industry. And the record industry will know who you are and what you're downloading."

The music industry has not been particularly concerned with knowing the details and intimate buying habits of its consumers, even though the average household spends about $270 yearly on music. The Web is all about knowing your clientele, and target-marketing to them. That's why artists are flocking away from the record companies in growing numbers.

Chuck D of Public Enemy was frustrated that Def Jam Records kept delaying the release of his *Bring the Noise 2000* album, so he posted some unreleased tracks in MP3 format on the Public Enemy Web site at *www.public-enemy.com.* Def Jam instructed him to stop. Instead, Public Enemy left Def Jam, which had issued every P.E. album since its 1987 debut, *Yo! Bum Rush the Show.*

Public Enemy's latest release, *There's a Poison Goin' On,* began its life online, with online label AtomicPop.com. Public Enemy now sees half the profits as opposed to less than 10 percent.

"Artists, particularly established ones, might try to carve out Internet rights for themselves in their renegotiations with conventional labels and that might become a serious issue," notes Al Teller, former CEO of MCA and founder of AtomicPop.com. "The traditional record companies will have their role confined to dealing with hard goods in offline space. They'll fight to retain all rights because most record contracts today call for exclusivity. There is going to be a lot of revisiting of the core fundamentals upon which the industry has been operating for quite some time. It's been brought upon us by virtue of the new Internet technologies."

According to research by Market Tracking International, Web sales will grow to 10–15 percent of the $47.5 billion music market by 2004.

The music industry has been fighting this shift of distribution economics because it will alter the whole economic structure of the industry, wiping out some record retailers virtually overnight. Remember: Record retailers are all set up with their stores, staff, and everything else—they have huge overheads that have to be covered. Business can't change overnight, but the industry, technology-wise, has gotten so sophisticated that it may very well do that. When that happens, the economic impact could be devastating.

"Retailers are going to have to change, because that day is coming," observes Tony Ferguson, who does A&R at Interscope Records. "If they don't catch on to the technology and figure out a way of utilizing it for their own good as salesmen, they are going to be out of business. Then all you'll have left is Blockbuster with video rentals. CDs may very well become a thing of the past, if they're not careful. Soon, we're going to have the ability to download music. We're approaching a ramp-up phase, a crossover time period. The technology is practically there. We're getting to the stage now where we don't want to use FedEx or messenger services to listen to mixes. I could be here in my office, and I could have a record being made in Australia downloaded over the phone lines into my computer, and I could hear the finished master. It's going to be a brave new world—that's for sure."

Already, every genre of music is getting a boost from the Web, whether it's jazz or New Age. This is happening because rock 'n' roll music appeals to kids, and the 27 million thirteen- to nineteen-year-olds in the United States love computers. Eighty-seven percent of these kids have access to online services, so they can find music on the Web. New Age, classical, and jazz aficionados are sophisticated, and they're early adopters of new technology. But the area that is really excelling on the Web is the niche music market.

In August 1999, record industry titan Rhino Records inaugurated Rhino Handmade, a Web-only imprint that issues limited-edition releases from Rhino-owned and -controlled archives. Rhino Handmade's smaller quantities and overhead permit it to release titles that might be deemed too esoteric for conventional distribution outlets. Rhino Handmade releases (each one individually numbered) are issued in quantities as small as 1,000 copies and are discontinued as soon as this initial run has sold out.

"It's one small step for a compact disc, one giant leap for collectors," exclaims Roland Worthington Hand, curator of the Rhino Handmade Institute of Petromusicology and chief archivist for Rhino Handmade. "We're going through all of our archives with a keen eye and ear and a fine-tooth comb to create surprising and astounding releases for music-loving 'Netizens' everywhere."

The label will have biweekly releases of material that is either out of print or that has never been released before. The releases include Rhino's first artist, Wild Man Fischer, a previously unheard 1982 album from Tower of Power, and a set of DEVO rarities. Albums are available exclusively online at the Rhino Handmade Web site, located at *www.rhinohandmade.com,* and are sold on a first-come, first-served basis.

# Getting Into Distribution

The vast majority of people in the distribution business started off in retail—in other words, they worked in record stores as kids.

"When I was doing it, it was very exciting—you actually sold records," recalls Dave Yeskel. "You developed relationships with your customers, you made music recommendations, you got people to make multiple purchases because you loved the music. It was the coolest job in the world to work in a record store."

After selling records to individuals, the next logical step up the ladder is to sell records for a distributor, or for a label. That's when you become what is called a field merchandising rep—that is, a foot soldier. You're the one in the stores—putting up posters, taking inventory, doing store reports, dropping off promos. As a field merchandising rep, your objective is to establish good relationships with as many stores as you possibly can in your territory.

"It was a great education," asserts Dave, who was a field merchandising rep in Philadelphia, southern New Jersey, and Delaware. "I learned how the record business worked."

Those in distribution find selling records to be the most satisfying aspect of the job.

"I really enjoy taking somebody who was nothing and making stars out of them," reveals Dave.

# Distributing Stars

Since distribution is all about getting your product to the marketplace, the difficulty lies in just how this is done. It's become incredibly competitive to get records into the stores. The music industry releases approximately 30,000 titles each year. The average record store holds 15,000–20,000—both new releases and old favorites. Because most stores can't carry every title, they often opt for the music that's an easy sell.

The idea behind carrying titles that will sell quickly—called "turning of inventory"—is that the more items you turn over, the more profit you will make. The philosophy of most retail outlets is to go for the guaranteed big turns. If the youth market is big, the retailer will want to stock quick-sell items like Ricky Martin, Britney Spears, the Backstreet Boys, and 'N Sync, knowing that the turnover will be fast and the profits high. As a distributor, you have to be prepared to provide retailers with the quick-sells they need, as well as the right product to meet the demands of their particular market.

Working in distribution takes a combination of enthusiasm for different brands of music, a mind for developing new markets, and plain old common sense. Whether working independently or for a large record company, your role in the music marketplace is essential and will be even more so in upcoming years with the rapid restructuring of the online economy. Be prepared, and get excited: As Dave Yeskel says, someday you'll be making stars.

# *Turn Up the Radio* ‖:

The guy on the radio is the me that lives inside, me un-governed, pure id with no ego, if you wanna put it in Freudian terms or whatever—the me I wish I was. I've always been kind of disturbed by the other guy.

—HOWARD STERN
KING OF ALL MEDIA

## Radio

*L*ots of people think disc jockeys live the good life—they have a four-hour workday, they get to stand onstage and announce bands, they get to pick songs. And they become famous even though nobody knows what they look like.

"I decided that radio was probably my kind of profession," offers Dan Ingram, a disc jockey for WCBS-FM (101.1) in New York City. "It's one where you have minimal involvement for maximum return."

A little history for you: The first commercial radio station started in 1920 as station KDKA, broadcasting from Pittsburgh. During the "golden years" of radio—the 1940s—radio personalities were paid as much as movie stars and treated with the same celebrity. Club disc jockeys reached their apex in the mid-1970s and early 1980s, when disco was the craze and nightclubbing was de rigueur for those in social circuits.

These days, breaking into broadcast radio is difficult. Aspiring DJs pursue auditions, running from radio station to radio station, actively self-promoting. They bring clippings, taped samples of their work, and recommendations to prospective employers. Many DJs take internships or menial jobs at radio stations to get themselves introduced to those who hire on-air talent. The hours are long and often unrewarding.

"It's kind of like being a drug dealer," quips DJ David X. "You hang around with the wrong crowd long enough and you pick it up. (I'm halfway kidding here.)"

If you're just starting out, the way to get into radio these days is by niche marketing, as opposed to going straight to a top radio station, a talk show station, or a news station. If this is where you want to go, get a lead in any way you can.

"I got into radio during my senior year in high school. I was in a radio class because I thought it would be easy," observes Sheryl Stewart, a disc jockey for Air 1 Christian stations. "I loved music from the time I was a small child. I used to sing along with my Mom and Dad's old Carpenters's record. I couldn't believe that there were actually people who would pay you to play music! It seemed like that was the job for me! My high school radio teacher was the P.D. of a Christian station in Salem, Oregon, and he offered me a part-time job when I graduated. I took it and ended up staying at that station for ten years."

As a female who was into Christian music, it was easy for Sheryl to find her niche. Of all radio professionals, only 15 percent are female. Being a woman gives Sheryl an immediate advantage because she's a novelty. To become someone in the radio business, a radio DJ must build an audience. Most specialize in a specific musical genre, have a consistent approach, and field calls and requests from interested listeners to develop a consistent, loyal listening public. Since only one person is usually on the air at a given time, the DJs get lonely. In surveys, over 75 percent mentioned "isolation" as one of the biggest drawbacks of the career.

Radio is also not a particularly well-paying field. The average starting salary in radio is about $12,000 a year. That grows to $25,000 after five years, and to $40,000 after a decade.

"I was working five days a week, doing Top 40 stuff, and having a good time, but I was getting almost no money," confirms Dan Ingram.

> **Commit it to memory:** It takes a lot of passion and many years of hard work to become a financially successful disc jockey.

# DJ Skills

There are no specific educational requirements to become a disc jockey. DJ'ing is a passion, and most radio disc jockeys start at college radio stations or in small markets; others intern while in school to learn the equipment used in the industry. Many create tapes of their shows and save clippings to use as introductions to professional radio stations. A radio jockey must be familiar with current or specialty (subgenre) musical trends and how specific songs fit together. He must be able to fill empty space with information and have a clear, clean speaking voice and a certain amount of technical skill.

Being fast on your feet is important. Besides playing music, you're expected to chat, deliver news, weather, or sports, or hold conversations with celebrities or call-in listeners. You need to be able to take an item in the news and relate it to a hot new song. DJs need to think about how things connect.

You know you're moving up the DJ ladder if you can support yourself and have earned at least secondary on-air responsibilities. If you're moving up, you're very busy between promotional stints, work, and keeping current on musical trends. Perhaps you've got contacts in the music business, and do some band scouting as well.

"The Eels were a band that I was playing the demo for at KCRW," recalls Chris Douridas, former music director and host of the KCRW radio program "Morning Becomes Eclectic" and current A&R contact at DreamWorks Records. "At my first interview at DreamWorks, I dropped the Eels demo to the heads of the label, and they proceeded to sign them a month later."

Over 60 percent of DJs rotate from one position in the radio industry to another, moving to news anchoring, call-in shows, specialty shows, and sports shows. Another 7 percent write copy for radio broadcasts, television broadcasts, and newspapers. Others expand into various areas of the music business.

"When my husband was transferred to Sacramento, I was able to get a job with K-LOVE," notes Sheryl Stewart. "From K-LOVE, I went to mainstream radio in Sacramento. I worked at the Zone [alternative] and Arrow 108 [classic rock]. I also did some work for KSSJ [smooth jazz], the End [Top 40], and KKSF in San Francisco [smooth jazz]. I had accepted a job doing morning news for Mix 96 [adult contemporary] when I decided to come work with Air 1."

## Dan Ingram's Story

For almost twenty-one years, Dan Ingram was known as the sound of afternoon-drive radio on WABC-AM in New York City. He got there by way of two radio comrades—Stan Kaplan and Bob Whitney. They had started a company called Mars Broadcasting in Stamford, Connecticut, and Dan left his other on-air work to become their production manager.

One of the stations to which Mars Broadcasting sold their monthly package of contests was WABC in New York. Because Dan was the guy who would bring the packages to the station, he had access to the general manager, a guy by the name of Hal Neal.

WABC had hired a new DJ who was not right for WABC's pop format. He did the show as if it were a kiddie show.

"I went into Hal's office one day to drop off some contests, and I said, 'You know, the guy who's on in the afternoon isn't helping you out,'" recalls Dan.

"Who do you think would be better?" Hal asked.

"Me!"

"I had two tapes with me," says Dan. "One was me on KBOX in Dallas and the other was me on WIL in St. Louis. I gave them to him, and he said he'd listen to my shows. Hal listened to them and said that he liked the tapes, but he didn't know how I'd sound on WABC."

"Then I'll have a tape on your desk tomorrow," Dan volunteered.

He went into the studio that evening and found an old air check that he had taken off WABC-FM, which in those days was simulcast. He cut out the guy who was on the tape, put himself in, and remixed the whole thing in two-track mono.

"Hal called and said, 'I like your tape. Meet me at the 5:49 train that arrives in Stamford.' We went into the bar at the Stamford railroad station and had a couple of drinks. He said he wanted me to do his afternoon show."

## Other Radio Positions

Behind the disc jockey are a host of other jobs. Among them is the program director. His job is to assist the general manager in the supervision and direction of the programming unit of the radio station. He manages four to six professional staff and seven to ten support staff. You need some experience to get to this point, generally three to four years in radio programming operations and an FCC Restricted Radio Telephone Operator Permit. A good program director will select a playlist that helps a radio station carve out a unique and profitable niche in the radio marketplace.

"When I started at ABC, Hal asked me to program the station for him," recalls Dan. "I told him that I didn't want to be program director, and he told me that he had just released the guy who had been consulting for him, Mike Joseph. I said, 'Fine.' I took the 220-record list and cut it down to about 40. I threw off all of the 'soaring' album cuts . . . got a new jingle package, put a little bit of echo on the signal—that sort of stuff."

Among other things, the program director's duties usually include:

- Analyzing audience data and making program decisions in response to audience analysis.
- Designing the program schedule.
- Determining programming and announcing guidelines.
- Monitoring station transmissions through systematic analysis to ensure that the program schedule is adhered to and assessing the quality of performance of the announcers; initiating action to ensure compliance with previously established standards.
- Participating in overall station management by assisting the general manager in developing policies and procedures related to programming.
- Supervising news, music, production, operations, and announcer units; providing administrative supervision, developing air-shift schedules, and conferring with staff to eliminate program duplication.
- Determining program selection and acquisition.
- Performing announcing duties, as required.

## Syndicating Radio Shows

If you're looking for big money in radio, follow the Howard Stern route: Syndicate your radio show. When K-ROCK hired Howard Stern back in the eighties, he spent the next few years rolling his program out to eighteen cities nationwide, getting onto cable, writing books, and becoming the self-proclaimed "King of All Media."

These days, everybody wants a piece of Stern. Primarily on the strength of his show, the CBS-Westinghouse radio group bought Infinity Broadcasting (which owns Stern's show) in 1996. His books, *Private Parts* and *Miss America,* have been published by Simon & Schuster and HarperCollins. He has a long-running show on the E! Entertainment cable station, and Paramount Pictures lets him make movies like *Private Parts.*

Stern's success has legitimized a chaotic, juvenile morning broadcast formula—one copied by rival stations in nearly every major market where Stern's show airs and in many more where it does not.

"He created a new format, and he's the only one who does it perfectly," says screenwriter Len Blum, who adapted *Private Parts* for the movies. "It's Howard Stern Radio."

"You can reasonably say that he has worn down resistance to his kind of humor," says Paul D. Colford, author of *Howard Stern: King of All Media,* an unauthorized biography. "Unfortunately, a disproportionate amount of it is cruel humor."

Syndication is definitely a growing trend. More and more radio stations are finding it cheaper to buy nationally syndicated shows rather than producing their own.

You don't just have to syndicate a personality; you can syndicate a radio service. Westwood One, Inc., promotes itself as America's largest radio network, providing over 150 news, sports, music, talk, and entertainment programs, plus features, coverage of live events, twenty-four–hour formats, and shadow broadcast services, including shadow traffic, news, and sports. Westwood One services more than five thousand radio stations around the world, and is managed by Infinity Broadcasting.

King Biscuit produces radio programming, including the classic rock radio archive "King Biscuit Flower Hour," which airs in more than 180 U.S. markets on a weekly basis. The company has more than 21,000 recordings with performances by such artists as Bruce Springsteen, the Rolling Stones, the Who, the Beach Boys, and Eric Clapton; the Silver Eagle Cross Country radio show; and four record company imprints—Oxygen, Pet Rock, Silver Eagle Cross Country, and KBFH.

In 1999, the King Biscuit Entertainment Group signed an exclusive licensing agreement with emusic.com to release dozens of titles from King Biscuit's four imprints, including classic live recordings from the "King Biscuit Flower Hour" archive, for download in the MP3 format.

## Going the Club Route

Club DJs mix music, sound effects, and special effects, and occasionally provide time-filling chatter between songs. These DJs must be in command of their specialty—genre of music or demographic of audience—and sensitive to listener responses.

A club disc jockey keeps regular hours, usually working from 8:00 P.M. to 4:00 A.M. They get into it mostly out of passion. And, for the record, most DJs don't socialize regularly with those who do not keep the same odd hours.

"My uncle taught skating lessons part-time on Saturday mornings," recounts DJ David X. "He'd ask me if I wanted to come along and help him out by playing music, and DJ the first public session after that, since the rink didn't have a DJ for that one. Well, it was only a bunch of little kids, but man it was cool! *I was hooked!*"

Next thing you know, you're getting home equipment to play with and learn on. A couple of belt-drive turntables with pitch control, a mixer, a mic/line mixer with cue, and, voilà! You're ready to start beat-mixing records.

"There came a point in my life where I had to decide if I wanted to do this for a living or just keep it as a hobby," recalls DJ David X. "Loving music like I do, it soon came to pass that I found myself doing this full-time for a living—a decision I do not regret—but it has definitely not been the easy road to travel!"

To survive and thrive, club DJs must keep the crowd interested in dancing, so they have to be familiar with a wide variety of styles and songs that appeal to different groups.

A club disc jockey must know how to mix beats so the music progresses smoothly, how to design a night of music around a specific theme or requested type of music, and how to use lighting and special effects to his advantage. To break in, many DJs work for free at established clubs on off nights.

"I've tried to keep myself in club gigs," offers David X. "I chose to do clubs because I have a very artistic approach to what I do, and I wanted a way to express my creativity with music. I have also met the rudest people to ever walk the face of the earth, as well as some great business contacts."

Close contact with record promoters is important in getting copies of unreleased demos or other songs that distinguish you from other DJs. A DJ trades on his reputation, so staying current with musical trends and responding to listener feedback are critical to success.

Record promoters and agents try to flood high-profile DJs with new albums, hoping to gain exposure for their acts. Over 40 percent of all DJs work part-time and find it difficult to land regular, reasonably well-paying gigs.

"There was a time when I had a full-time day job," confirms David X. "I still work a day job, but now only part-time. It's difficult not to, especially in Sacramento, where I live. If you want to be a DJ at any level, it becomes a labor of love. You *will* find a way if you want to bad enough, just like anything else."

Many club DJs move to large urban centers to find a market that will support their services, but it's still difficult to get hired initially without a following that you can be expected to draw to the club.

"I have had some of my most euphoric moments working a crowd into a frenzy," shares David X. "It's a completely natural high, rivaled by nothing!"

DJs who have survived the club circuit for ten years are on the back end of their careers, because the life is rigorous and it's rarely forever. The connections a ten-year DJ has provide him with ample opportunity to enter the record industry, the promotion industry, or the club-managing scene.

## Digital DJ

British DJ Richard Eden doesn't have to truck singles from one club to another. As one of the first all-digital DJs, Eden carries his entire collection of dance, trance, dub, and jungle in one hand, on his Dell Inspiron 3200 laptop.

"I can select tracks very quickly," Eden notes. "With vinyl, CD, and MiniDisc, you have to search for the particular item [and] place it into the player. With MP3s, you click and the track is immediately available."

Eden compiles his premiere all-digital set by downloading almost half the music from sites such as MP3.com and Crunch. The remainder of his set consists of promotional CDs ripped with Music Jukebox or a basic MP3 encoder. Vinyl purists may balk, but Eden contends that laptop DJs have a number of advantages.

"They can choose and find tracks quickly, overlap tracks quickly, link into a drum machine on the computer," he notes. "It really just opens up what a DJ can do without having to prepare as much, which can only benefit the sound the DJ produces and, in turn, the audience's enjoyment."

# MARKETING AND PROMOTION: *Shake Your Money Maker*

SoundScan has made tracking record sales a precise art—the concept of actually marketing and promoting and selling it is not.

—DAVE YESKEL, VICE PRESIDENT OF SALES
WINDHAM HILL GROUP OF LABELS

## Hand in Hand

*M*arketing and promotion are two separate elements that work together to raise an artist's popularity. In essence, promotion is part of marketing, but everything is very departmentalized at a record company. You have a promotion department. You have a marketing department. You have a sales department. You have a publicity department. Even though marketing is the umbrella of everything that is done, the record label separates it.

"When you're talking about promotion, you're talking about radio promotion, getting the record on radio stations. Marketing is basically exposing an artist through free avenues—free being press and radio airplay," explains Bob Chiappardi, president and CEO of Concrete Marketing.

To excel in marketing or promotion, you need a salesman's personality—a lot of persistence, smiling, shaking hands, and cheering—not to mention a willingness to endure your fair share of late nights. The satisfying aspect of this work is that the results are tangible—radio airplay, media coverage—things that make the artist and the management ooohh and ahhh.

"After Hollywood Records began our marketing and promotion campaign for *Mr. Funny Face* we became very visible," observes Steve Summers, vocalist for the band Sprung Monkey. "I opened a local magazine in San Diego and I saw a full-page ad. There was this total blitz on the radio—three powerhouse stations. For two weeks before the album came out all you heard about on the radio was Sprung Monkey. I'm sure they bought a lot of ads to do that, which was incredible."

"To break a band it is always a combination of elements," explains Tom Barsanti, senior vice president and general manager at Jeff McClusky & Associates, an independent radio promotion company. "The music has to be there for it to work. If the music is good, then the marketing and promotion pays off. Once the exposure is there, the song can take off. A hit record without marketing will be tough—it will have a struggle, but marketing without a hit record won't make any difference."

"Marketing and publicity involves putting together a campaign, working with that band, and working with the team that promotes the band to radio," notes Kathy Acquaviva. "Bigger bands that have more access to radio help promote all areas of marketing. It makes all aspects easier because radio is such a driven side of the business."

It varies from label to label as to which department has the bigger budget. "Budgets are dispersed depending on the company," confirms Dave Yeskel. "Are you a marketing-intensive company or are you a promotion-intensive company? There are specific guidelines that say a certain percentage should be spent on marketing and a certain percentage should be spent on promotion, but it varies from company to company."

"When I first came to Century Media, I came from a publicity background. I was highly into the idea that you need a lot of press and you need a lot of radio," says Marco Barbieri. "If you don't have the records available, it doesn't really help. We became extremely sales aggressive. When we shifted the focus, we started executing different marketing and promotion ideas, and it went great. Now we make five times the income we did three years ago just because we opened up to so many different possibilities. This, in turn, increases our marketing by creating more hype for the label and more interest from the press, and more spins on the radio."

Press, as a rule, does not sell a lot of records, but increases familiarity with the act. Radio airplay, touring, and TV have proven to be more effective ways of selling music. Internet statistics are still being compiled. The quickest way to sell a lot of records is to have a hit record on radio and a video on MTV. The problem is this: Only a handful of records ever get that far.

# Marketing and Promotion Strategies

When planning a marketing and promotion campaign for a band, the record company needs to think about:

1. Radio promotion
2. Tour support
3. Videos

Sometimes, record company executives won't invest in a video until they see if this song is going to be a hit. If they have faith in the project, they may allocate video promotion dollars.

Marketing a band is a big project. You're talking $500,000 to do the job properly—and that doesn't include advertising. This may sound like a healthy chunk of change, with a myriad of uses, but in all actuality it isn't.

Let's say you want to have a group like the Beastie Boys go to London for press promotion. Because every member of the band is recognizable, it can't be just a lead singer; it has to be all three members of the band. Putting a band up in London for three to four nights is an expensive proposition—$350 per night per room. And while the Beasties are there, the record company is inevitably going to throw a party on their behalf—there goes another $10,000. A label can burn up so much money that artists often feel that they should be getting more money from record sales. But a complete publicity campaign is expensive, and the expenses the record company puts out on the first album can be recouped on the third album.

The major labels make huge investments on bands, so the number of units they have to sell is huge. An artist could wind up with a platinum album on the third record and it wouldn't even make back all the marketing dollars the record company spent on the three albums to arrive at platinum. Being a successful major label artist is a tough business—only one act in ten makes a profit, but that superstar recoups enough money to make up for the other nine.

# How Marketing and Promotion Help

Let's analyze the marketing and promotion of a make-believe band. We'll call them Smarty Boots. Their music is hard rock, with a little bit of alternative and electronica thrown in for good measure. The publicist's job starts three or four months before the album is released. It's the publicist's responsibility to begin marketing the artist by sending out advance copies of the album to the media.

Then radio promotion starts. Radio is all about relationships and promotion budgets. The bigger your promotion budget, the more airplay should result. Once the song is on the radio, a publicist's job gets much easier.

Now, when a publicist goes back to the media for round two and says, "Hi! I'm calling to follow up on that Smarty Boots CD we sent you. It's been a couple of months since we last spoke, and the song 'Boys or Men' is now getting airplay. It's on thirty to fifty radio stations—a combination of rock and alternative around the country—and it's starting to really take."

A strong pitch backed by statistics should definitely prompt a response from the media; after all, they're always looking for ways to keep a story up to date, as a magazine's lead time might be two to three months before it actually hits the newsstands. Still, it may not entice the critical intelligentsia, which encompasses *Rolling Stone, Spin, Musician, Time,* and *Newsweek*—the gatekeepers of taste. Their support is imperative for universal acceptance.

Of course, the gatekeepers of taste are not an easy sell; they have a limited amount of space for a lot of talent. Looking for another out, the journalist inquires, "Are they touring?"

The chain reaction starts, and the marketing and promotion machine revs up. The publicist says to the label, "The press is asking about a tour."

Now the marketing department has to consider what encompasses marketing and what constitutes promotion. Is it tour support? Is it in the budget? If the answer is yes, monies will be channeled into marketing and promoting the band on tour. With radio airplay and a tour in the works, Smarty Boots has about a one-in-ten chance of making moneymaking music. Nobody is a guaranteed success.

> **Commit it to memory:** *What makes one band a hit over another group is the marketing—how cleverly an act is spun and positioned.*

## Radio Promotion

Radio isn't essential to break a band, but it sure makes it easier. Record labels still rely heavily on radio airplay to expose consumers to music by new artists and to stimulate record sales. The exposure generated by a radio hit can increase album sales dramatically, transforming unknown acts, such as No Doubt and the Spice Girls, into multimillion-selling pop stars.

"If you want to break your record into radio, you have to utilize our services to make sure that the record gets played at the proper amount of stations—you know, gets the proper amount of spins, and the proper attention it needs," advises James Schureck, director of new media for Jeff McClusky & Associates, which is the biggest U.S. indie for Top 40 and alternative radio.

Any record company that is promotion driven has a two-tiered strategy: The first step is for the label to have its own promotion team in-house; the second is to use independent radio promoters—"indies," as they are known in the industry. (FYI: Record companies that rely heavily on independent radio promoters have promotion budgets that are significantly larger than their marketing budgets.)

Lots and lots of money in the record company budget goes into radio promotion. How this works is a well-shrouded mystery shared by few more than the promotion people, the radio promoters, and the radio station.

## Indies

Hypothetically, radio is an open market, and it should be free—but there is a fair amount of leverage, bribery and payola that goes into getting a song on the radio. If you want to see it, just become an indie.

"There are three major labels and there are a handful of big indie labels, and all of them call every radio programmer every week telling them they've got a great song . . ." explains James Schureck. "Who is the programmer to believe? We filter out a lot of that. Programmers trust what we say because we don't steer them wrong—we give them an unbiased opinion."

Radio indies are people who have spent a lot of their lives in the radio business. They have great relationships and they have networks of stations that will follow their lead. Indies spread the word and make life easier. Generally speaking, a great song is not going to immediately find twenty to forty radio stations on its own without the help of an indie.

"If you get an ad at a commercial radio station, you are guaranteed the record is going to be spun almost continuously, around the clock," points out Kathy Callahan of Windham Hill Records. "Once a radio station takes on a song, they pound the record. It's worth a lot."

Record companies give millions of dollars each year to this tiny clique of independent promoters, who pay annual lump sums to key stations, sponsor contests with large prizes for programmers, publish trade tip sheets, and hand out freebies.

"When a record gets played on the radio, we don't get paid anything," asserts Dave Yeskel. "The label gets it on the back end by selling the records, unless, of course, the record company owns the publishing company, which a lot of them do."

Indies contend that they can influence radio airplay, though how they do so is unclear since it is illegal to trade money or gifts for airplay. While it is not illegal for a station to take money in exchange for playing a song, it is illegal to accept money for playing a specific song without disclosing the payment to the public.

"We work records depending upon who's paying us—that's a big factor. Also if it's a good record," James notes. "You listen to a record and you can tell if it's going to be a hit. You do a lot of research. For example, if KROQ in L.A. or the EDGE in Phoenix adds a record, they're usually an indicator station. They seem to come on records early and 70 percent of the records they end up playing become hits in the rest of the country."

An indie tests the record in the marketplace by using various techniques:

1. Callout research: Calling people and asking what they think of the record
2. Focus groups: A hand-chosen target audience who gives feedback on songs
3. SoundScan: Charts album sales

The indie incorporates this information together with input from various key radio stations.

Another tactic indies use to get a song played is leverage. The theory is this: Convince the radio station that they've got a lot of advertisements from the label, so they want to play the new record. Most commercial radio stations work that way—one hand washes the other.

"I've known it to happen," observes radio veteran Chris Douridas. "It's unfortunate, the way it's happening now. It's much more difficult to detect than it was in the past because there are all sorts of ways of hiding the reality."

According to James Schureck, indies work every record they're paid to, but some records get worked more than others. That's based on:

1. Money
2. If it's going to be a hit
3. If there is a history with the person who hired us on that record
4. If there is a history with the management
5. If there is a history with the artist

Indies have so much power that it has become difficult to determine just who is setting the agenda these days at radio: the program directors or the advertising sales managers.

# Britney Spears, for Example . . .

Let's take the story of teen phenomenon Britney Spears and how she broke into radio. To begin with, she was media ripe. When she made her debut, Britney Spears was a cute seventeen-year-old girl with a proven writing staff behind her on a major label. The music was tested in odd time slots on obscure radio stations. Feedback was positive. Next, the indie went around and set up radio shows. More positive feedback. Listeners asked to hear Britney Spears.

"Certain stations know we try not to lead them wrong, so they'll add records," confides James Schureck. "Once you get enough stations adding the record, then the bigger stations say, 'Enough of the smaller stations have come in; I think I'm going to take a chance with this record.' They give it a few rotations throughout the week and see what kind of calls come in from the audience. The more response, the more they'll spin it."

It took several months, but once Britney Spears started getting into the public consciousness, the indies told their stations, "Listen to the music. We guarantee it's going to be a hit."

Britney took months. Ricky Martin exploded in a couple of weeks with "Livin' la Vida Loca." Proof positive that there's no proven formula for a new song's acceptance in radio.

# Positioning an Artist

"The real hothouse for the record business right now is in the area of marketing," states Bud Scoppa, vice president of A&R for the Sire Records Group. "If you look at some of the most noteworthy success stories of breaking artists over the last few years, you'll see that these breakthroughs are predicated on creative marketing to a significant degree. One example that I think is noteworthy is Atlantic's work in the initial stages of the Jewel project. They had her out doing regional residencies in coffeehouses in various parts of the country over a period of months. They were really patient as a series of scattered small buzzes in various parts of the country eventually coalesced into a snowball effect.

"Hit records aren't made in marketing meetings. They're made in the studio. Fiona Apple's debut album was a great album, but Jeff Ayeroff, the copresident of Sony/Work Records, made a great marketing campaign that broke her."

Any artist—Jewel, Alanis Morissette, Fiona Apple—has to be positioned in the music marketplace so consumers don't confuse one with another. How an artist is positioned is an outgrowth of meeting with the artist, the artist's manager, and everybody in the record company who's going to be involved with selling the album.

The people who are the heads of the departments and who are going to handle the artist—whether in radio promotion, marketing, sales, or internationally—everybody in the company that holds a decision-making seat will sit down and hash it out: How should this record go? Where should this be positioned? Who is this artist and to whom does she appeal? What do we need to do to find their customer base?

"When you're figuring out the marketing plan for an artist, you brainstorm," observes Dave Yeskel. "Some projects lend themselves to obvious ideas; other times it gets very creative. You think about new ways of doing things: What connections can be made between the themes of the record and the artwork or the title? What larger company with a lot of money would like to get exposed to a different audience, and would pay to be on our posters and samplers?"

Once the label figures out how to position the artist, the label then analyzes that talent's sales potential. Label executives figure out how much money they can afford to spend getting the word out while still making a profit. That's how they arrive at the marketing budget. The rate is usually $1–$1.50 in marketing for every album the label anticipates selling. Budgets are all based on sales projections.

## The Marketing Campaign

Marketing people are responsible for creating an identity for the music—then they find ways to get that identity and the music out to the public. The objective is to sell albums through exposure. Marketing involves a lot of creativity—acts are promoted in a vast variety of conceivable and inconceivable ways.

"It's taking everything the artist and the project has to offer and trying to find hooks and angles," notes Dave Yeskel, who considers his job to be as much about marketing as it is about distribution. "We do samplers, we do tie-ins with third-party companies to leverage our brand and our artists. We get them on the radio. We put them on tour. We get them on TV when humanly possible. You have to get people to hear it. It has to make that emotional connection before people will buy it."

Statistics state that the average person has to hear and see a band's name eight times before the group's name registers. This means the marketing department has to create fan awareness, because if no one knows a band is out there, there's no way they're going to build a following.

Easy inexpensive ways for promoting an artist include the Web, posters, concert listings, and even those flyers bands put under windshield wipers at concerts.

**Commit it to memory:** *An average person has to hear and see a band's name eight times before the group's name starts to register.*

When consumers hear a single on the radio that they like, it registers, but since most of the time the disc jockey doesn't announce that song, they end up wondering, "Oh, what's that song? It's something about old photographs." Then, they're reading an article about the hit single "Wrinkled Pictures" and the lightbulb goes on. Publicity strengthens awareness of the band name and what they're all about, and it gives fans an opportunity to get to know them a bit better.

"You might buy it because you saw it on the cover of a magazine, you might buy it solely because you heard it on the radio. Publicity puts it all together and helps emphasize that band," affirms Laura Cohen, manager of publicity for Virgin Records.

## Niche Marketing

Concrete Marketing was formed in 1984 to promote hard rock. "The record companies didn't really understand the music, and the only way they would promote it was around radio airplay, and in the beginning heavy metal didn't get any airplay," recalls Bob Chiappardi. "We devised very street-oriented ways of getting the music out to the kids directly, using retail promotions, underground radio shows, and specialty shows on radio—among other things."

Concrete learned that a lot of radio shows weren't even getting serviced with hard rock albums. And if they were, the program director would get a record, see some gruesome thing on the cover, and bring it home to his kid who liked heavy metal music. "We were like the guys who mowed the lawn," recalls Bob. "It was much easier for the labels to pay somebody to promote hard rock rather than to sweat out there with a lawnmower."

## Marketing and Promotion Relationships

When you're doing marketing and promotion right, you're perceived as a hero because you're helping a band with their career. It leads to long-term relationships with bands, lots of gold records on the wall, and plenty of job satisfaction.

"Metallica has been a great long-term marketing relationship," contends Bob Chiappardi. "We started work with them very early on; we were doing stuff the record labels didn't have the savvy to do. We dealt with a lot of promotions and in-stores, contests and word of mouth. We developed a bunch of new ways to market Metallica and got those ideas working well. Even as the genre grew, and the record labels started understanding how to do it, they still hired us because we have a long-term understanding and relationships with bands, and that's been good.

"I like sitting down with a new artist and just developing a plan to expose the artist in a proper way," notes Bob Chiappardi. "Taking something that's a challenge—that is not going to get airplay and is not going to get any immediate recognition from the media—and building a groundswell with the kids is very satisfying because you build something on your own. Bands like Pantera and White Zombie were really doing well before the media embraced them. It's very rewarding. I've always been into helping young bands."

# Art Direction

The responsibility of designing the look and feel of an album and a marketing and promotion campaign falls on the art director. This is a really pleasant and not particularly well-paying area of the music business.

Unless it's a big-name act, the musicians generally don't get to do their own art. The art department works with the act on their packaging campaign. Thus, creating an album cover, as well as the posters and promotions to go with it, is a joint effort. The labels maintain a fair amount of control over what an artist's album will look like because they want to be able to sell it in Wal-Mart.

"The process is different every time I do a cover," admits Robert Fisher, former art director at Geffen Records and Geffen DGC. "I try to spend a healthy amount of time with the band, getting to know them and getting a feel for what they're about. I get the music to listen to the band and try to see them live. You have to get into what the artist is about and try to express that vision."

Once an artist finishes a record, the art director has about four months to create the album cover and the accompanying promotional material.

You may think designing a cover is a relatively simple process, but there are a lot of details involved. Has the band thought about the inside-CD booklet? The standard format for this booklet is three panels, six sides—basically a three-page pullout. Does the group want the standard foldout, or a booklet with pages stapled in the center? Should it be a long foldout or the kind of thing that unfolds into a little poster? Seemingly trivial decisions, but they have to be made nonetheless.

For an art director, it's important to draw from the band ideas about style and personality, then bring aboard the appropriate people to complete that vision. Photographers and graphic designers all have their own little styles and niches and are not appropriate for all artists.

"On our first record I was under the impression, 'Well, the label has an art department—they'll pick out photographers, they'll pick out record designers. They know more about it than I do,'" notes Scott Lucas, frontman for the platinum band Local H. "When you do that, it may turn out fine, but I don't think it reflects the personality of the band.

"This job is so much fun," concludes Robert Fisher. "When we'd do a photo shoot, we have to consider dressing the studio with props and backdrops and that kind of stuff. There's also styling and wardrobe. Some bands are fine on their own—they have great clothes—sometimes they need some assistance. Sometimes we bring hair and makeup for people if they need it. Gotta love doing fun things like that."

# PRODUCTION:

## *Minute with the Maker* ‖:

I just think I have the skills to produce, so I'm doing it.

—FIELDY, BASS PLAYER

KORN

*M*any people have a hand in the final CD that you put in your music system. Of people in all these positions, none is as important as the producer.

Producers enjoy the process of making a record. They usually are musicians or engineers who have evolved as they have risen through the ranks. They know how to arrange songs, and how to use a studio. They revel in hearing a music track fall into place or the emotional performance of a vocalist. To a producer, when a band is on top of the creative process, it's a magical moment.

"A good producer will make a band's music sound cleaner and more unique," declares producer JJ French, a former member of the platinum heavy metal band Twisted Sister. "A record producer is someone who loves the creative process. You're very close to the music; it's very, very satisfying."

A producer should have skills in four key areas:

1. The science of sound and engineering—finding sounds and getting them to tape
2. The art of songwriting and arranging

3. An aptitude for working closely with people in creative situations for long periods of time
4. The business side of making music

The producer guides the creative direction of a music project, just as a film director guides a movie project. Ron Howard and the Coen Brothers might take the same script and make radically different movies because their styles are so different. Similarly, the same song in the hands of two different record producers might end up sounding like two completely different tunes.

"The producer isn't really in charge. We know how we'd like our individual instruments to sound," observes guitarist Eddie Van Halen. "The producer is basically an outside, objective ear who suggests things, arrangement-wise and song-wise."

As a producer, you can have your fingers in any and all kinds of music—pop, R&B, jazz, soul, funk, punk, folk, country, rap, reggae, world, bagpipes, classical, traditional, Gregorian chant, cartoon, gospel, commercial, film scores, CD-ROM interactive, musicals, and children's. You name it, you can do it.

## The Production Process

A typical album recording usually starts with the producer listening to all of the songs an artist has available for the album. The producer's duty in choosing the songs is to satisfy the following folks:

1. The artist
2. The record company
3. The public

The next step would be to hire the sound engineer and, together with the artist, choose a recording studio that fits the atmosphere and budget of the project.

In the studio, the producer handles all the logistics (including money), while "directing" the musicians and the sound engineer to deliver the quality needed for the end result.

> **Commit it to memory:** The job of the producer is to help the musicians achieve their musical goals.

## Learning to Be a Producer

Most producers learn by doing.

"There are a few good recording schools, but if I were you I would save all that tuition money and use it to buy some good books, an 8-track machine, a mixer, and some mics, move into a house with a soundproof basement, and start learning by doing it," advises Seattle-based punk producer Jack Endino, who has produced discs for the likes of Nirvana, Mudhoney, and Skin Yard, among others.

Areas of study that will help you in your production work include physics, science, and electronics. If you're going to be hanging around a recording studio, it also helps if you've played at least one instrument. That way you know how to deal with each situation, whether it's drum tuning, guitar amp knob tweaking, dealing with different kinds of speakers, strings, and the like—all the hardware and the physics of it.

"I've been playing music since I was six years old," notes engineer Bob Rice. "I understand what the needs of musicians are because I am one, and these are the same needs I have. I need to be in a state of readiness when something fails, or to troubleshoot problems before they happen, or to prevent them from happening."

## What Is Expected of a Producer

The specifics of what a producer does are varied. On any given project, he may perform any or all of the following tasks:

- Act as a referee if two members of a band disagree about a song or instrumentation.
- Help choose which songs should be recorded for an album.
- Encourage an artist to rewrite, add parts, or delete parts of a song.
- Suggest different arrangements for a song.
- Control (either directly or by hiring an engineer) the sonics of a record—that is, digital recording versus analog, Dolby versus non-Dolby, this microphone versus that one, this guitar amp versus that one.
- Create an environment in which the artists will give their best performance. This can take a variety of approaches—bringing in candles or carpets, even making an artist angry while recording to capture the spirit of a song.

Producers are also sometimes held responsible for making sure that the album is completed on time and within budget. But this isn't the producer's primary function; frequently the administrative aspects of making a record are handled by project coordinators, not the producers themselves.

# Getting into Production

Usually, you start your production career on the road—playing, teching, whatever.

"I learned my production skills by doing a lot of roadie work," recalls Bob Rice. "The first tour I went on was with Frank Zappa in 1988—it was his last tour. I took care of a computer music system called the Synclavier. I had studied computer music in college, and they had a smaller version of the Synclavier, so I was basically able to teach myself how to operate that machine. That was the centerpiece of what I was doing for Frank Zappa, once he got his polytronic sampling system. In 1988 he decided he wanted to go on tour, and I had to take care of $750,000 in computer equipment that never belonged on the road. That's what taught me how to deal with computer hardware."

Jack Endino locked himself in a basement with a 4-track, and produced everything within earshot . . . including legendary Seattle bands like Green River. The only way to become a producer is to be around music—producers are former artists, engineers, musicians, and just plain music lovers. In other words, anyone with an ear for music can be a record producer.

"To be a good producer you have to study, like you study anything you're interested in," notes JJ French. "Spend time in the studio, get comfortable with it. You have to totally know songs. You don't necessarily have to know the console, but you should know what you want to hear."

The producer works with the artist in making decisions about the music. You need to be confident enough to say, "No, this guitar part does not work," or "This drum sound is not right for this song," and "Let's try this instead." In the studio, you get to be a knob tweaker, you get to play with a lot of different types of sounds, and you have a lot of tools at your disposal. If you're inclined to play with the music, the studio is the place to do it.

"I've always taken that edge, even in our band, Korn," bass player Reg "Fieldy" Arvizu points out. "I was supposed to produce Limp Bizkit's record, but we were touring and I was too busy. I couldn't do it. When I did Crown of Thorns I was actually too busy, but I understood what they wanted to do, so I made it happen."

It is necessary for a producer to have a vision of how the music should sound when it's finished. Having chosen a musical destination, the producer can then chart a course to that destination and help the band deliver a musical opus that can be enjoyed for years to come.

**Commit it to memory:** *A producer must have a vision of where the music is going.*

# Production Time

There is no job structure to being a producer. Sessions can be scheduled any time of day or night, or you may work continuously. It is not unusual for a producer to spend twenty hours in the studio to perfect one recording. About one-third of that time is spent doing the mix. All the recorded elements must be mixed down from twenty-four or forty-eight tracks to the final product: two-track stereo.

# A Producer's Relationship with the Band

As a producer, you need to have a positive relationship with the band. You need to understand them, get into their musical groove, listen to what they're trying to say musically, and help them say it better. A good producer presents a group with various sound options to try, shows them possibilities. A producer is an objective outsider when necessary, but always a friend and mentor.

"You can only produce a band effectively if you've earned the band's trust," notes George Drakoulias, who's signed and produced the Black Crowes, the Jayhawks, and the Freewheelers, among others. "You become very friendly with them and you gain their trust. You court the band, you talk to them, you spend a lot of time with them. You discuss records you like, records they like, then you talk about the songs. So by the time you start recording, they trust you, they know where you're at. They know you're not just saying something because you have to be right about everything. You're expressing an opinion because that is your opinion."

In the case of JJ French, the gold-selling band Sevendust had more faith in him as a producer and a manager than he had himself.

"To judge a producer, you listen to the CD," advises Lajon Witherspoon, the lead vocalist for Sevendust. "You listen to the CD on really good systems and bad systems, analyzing the work of the engineer and the producer. We also look to see if the guy we want to work with is the producer or the executive producer. A lot of these guys come in, and take the band's sound and make it a little better than what it normally is. JJ goes above and beyond."

"It's funny," laughs JJ. "When Sevendust asked me to get involved, I'd been out of the music business for a while. My wife had just had a baby, so I said, 'I really don't want to manage you guys, but I'd like to try my hand at producing.' They said yes. I loved the music they were playing. I had a real understanding, a real feel for it—we were on the exact same wavelength. So, I worked really closely with my coproducer, Mark Mendoza, to make a great record."

## A Producer and the Label

When a producer agrees to do an album, pleasing the band is the most important thing. Pleasing the label is next. It's a good idea for you to talk to the label people and find out just what sort of record they are expecting.

"If I can make both band and label happy, I will," contends Jack Endino. "If the band and the label have drastically different ideas, it's a bad scene and you should avoid it like the plague. As a producer, you should envision possible tension before you take the gig, or you may later become someone's scapegoat."

Sometimes the producer is expected to be the mediator between band and record label over song choices. This isn't a big deal in the indie marketplace, but when it comes to the major labels, and their insistence on packaging an artist, there can be some tension. It's not like it used to be in the days when the music business was more centralized. These days, most of the major label people respect the artist and seem to trust the producer's judgment without interfering in the record making process too much.

Case in point: When Steve Albini produced Nirvana's *In Utero* album, the follow-up to the 6 million–selling disc *Nevermind,* Nirvana frontman Kurt Cobain was determined not to make *Nevermind II,* and wanted to go off in a completely different direction. Nirvana's label, DGC, wanted *Nevermind II.* DGC was risking a lot of money—and the more money a label puts up to record a band, the greater potential for interference. As an independent producer, you are hired by the band, not the label. But your goal is to make everyone happy, which is what Steve did.

## Producer Money

A record producer usually is paid a production fee for his work plus a royalty on each record sold. Those fees may be as small as $1,000 per song for a new producer and upwards of $50,000 per song for the successful proven hit makers. Royalties may range from 1 percent to 8 percent for heavyweights like Bob Ezrin, Steve Albini, and Mutt Lange. The major labels will spend big money on a producer.

## The Engineer

Only second to the producer is the recording engineer. At minimum, he is a knob-turner, and at maximum, a scientist of sound. He may not yet be good enough to call himself a producer, or perhaps he doesn't want the responsibility. Maybe he's too much of a specialist, someone who has found his niche and excels in it.

The engineer is crucial to the recording process, but the producer gets all the credit. Most producers start as engineers and evolve into producers.

There are some producers who are not engineers, and lots more who used to be engineers but now hire engineers to assist them, but most of them at least know enough about engineering to know how to get sounds. Some very good producers are experienced musicians who've made a lot of records and who know which engineers to hire to be their hands and ears.

"Engineering is always a lot of fun," says Bob Rice. "In the studio, you get to be a knob-tweaker and that's one of my addictions/strengths. With studio playing, you get to play with a lot of different types of sounds, and you have a lot of tools at your disposal."

People who know how to operate the equipment in a recording studio and make a recording can call themselves recording engineers, but really good ones will find the world beating a path to their door. If they are indeed producer material, the world will let them know.

"When I went into the studio with Sevendust, I didn't have that much experience tweaking the sound," admits JJ French. "I knew what I wanted to hear, and I had a coproducer and an engineer who handled the technical stuff. I never touched the console."

# Mixing

When an engineer mixes an album, he is assembling the final two-track stereo versions from the multitrack masters. This is quite a process, as she's mixing together up to forty-eight tracks of sound into just the final two tracks that people will be able to listen to on their stereos.

The word "mixing" means two different things in the context of audio recording:

1. Adjusting the fader levels, balance, equalization, and the like so that the live sound is properly recorded in the first place
2. The art of turning the live sound recorded in step 1 into a finished, polished masterpiece that's ready to listen to.

Mixing down from multiple tracks to stereo is the second step of the process involved in making a finished song. All tracks on a multitrack recorder are mono by themselves. The mixing board is the central control unit in any recording studio.

When the engineer mixes down to stereo, he does the following for each track:

• Selects where in the stereo field he wants to hear it
• Selects how loud he wants to hear it
• Selects what effects and EQ he wants it to have

The mixing process allows the engineer to control the individual level of each instrument sent to tape, to control the tone of the instrument via equalization, or EQ, as well as the amount of effect being added to each instrument from the peripheral effect processors. As few as four instruments or microphones may be plugged in, or as many as forty-eight, and each one can be controlled individually.

Mixing is where all the hard decisions get made, and it can make the difference between a workmanlike recording and a masterpiece of sound . . . even when you start with the same source material.

The engineer has to have a feel for the abstract "ideal average stereo" out there in the real world, and his most important job is to make sure that the record will sound great on the maximum number of stereo systems.

Mixing is an intense and subjective process, and it's hard to maintain absolute consistency throughout a project. When mixing, your ears and perceptions will change slightly during the course of the project: Songs mixed at different times may sound very different in tone or in relative volume from one time to the next. Each song may sound fine by itself, but one may be subjectively louder than the next, making that following song seem smaller than it should; or your ears may get fatigued and the mixes slowly get brighter and brighter as your ears lose sensitivity to the high frequencies.

Mastering is the process of compressing or limiting the entire mix so that the levels on the mix as a whole are more consistent and even. The mastering engineer makes the sound consistent both tonally and volume-wise, so that a rock song is not quieter than the preceding acoustic guitar song, or one song is not duller sounding than the others. Mastering also involves some final tweaking to the EQ or editing songs so there's the correct amount of space between them, and so on.

Mastering is a very important part of getting that "radio ready" sound. Veteran engineers, or master engineers, make a CD as loud as possible without changing the sound of the music too obviously. All bands want to get as close as they can to the maximum digital output level (known as "digital zero") so their music will sound louder than everyone else's on the radio. This is a very tricky, exacting job, requiring some very high-powered digital processing gear and much care.

Mastering engineers usually have their own control rooms, called mastering suites, and never work anywhere else, because this allows them to really get to know how the sound in their room relates to the rest of the world. Once they know how things should sound in their room, they can make decisions quickly and with confidence.

# Your Own Studio

There are two sides to any argument, including whether or not producers should have their own studio. The upside for Jack Endino of not having his own studio is that he has been able to make records in ten countries. If he owned a studio, he could never leave; he'd always be recording there.

There are obvious benefits to having your own studio, such as getting to know how the room sounds and being able to utilize the characteristics of the room for the best sound possible.

"The biggest influence in shaping my style was a room," admits scoring mixer John Richards. "C.T.S. Studio 1 in London was where I began my career. The room was designed in the early sixties to meet the then-current trend of maximum separation between the sections of the orchestra, and had consequently an extremely short decay time. Records made at C.T.S. during that period had a very identifiable quality to the sound. Therefore, it was the studio—more than any one person—that helped me shape my style."

For many producers, having a studio allows them to work with groups they wouldn't normally be able to work with because there wasn't enough in the budget to hire a producer *and* book a studio.

"For someone like me who finds talent and develops it, it's important to be able to run into the studio and see if it works," notes producer Steve Addabbo. "We can do a couple of tracks, and if we like each other, we'll do it. If not, we'll go our own ways. It's the quickest way of finding out if a musical relationship is going to work. So, for me, having my own studio has been an invaluable tool to keeping my career going, because I'm able to go and develop new things without having to go and hire another studio. The overhead takes care of itself with other bookings."

Finding artists early in their careers and bringing them along has been the cornerstone of Steve's career.

# The Finished Product

"Being done with a record is very satisfying," admits Steve Addabbo. "Satisfying is when people respond, you hear it on the radio, people like what you've done. That's very satisfying. They say, 'That record really makes it,' or 'I listen to that record all the time.' That's the kind of thing you like to hear and you go, 'Wow! I really did something.'

"When you're in the middle of it, you don't know. You're working on it and you hope that it's good, you hope people will hear it."

# ON TOUR:
# *Wherever I May Roam* 𝄇

We need a Q-tip stage left. Paul's got something in his ear.
—SCOTT NORDVOLD, STAGEHAND
KISS

S teel cables dangle from the ceiling, which will eventually support five tons of speakers and a lighting rig that could double as a jungle gym for Godzilla. "See all the glamour?" deadpans Kiss rigger Erik Smith between sips of chocolate milk. "See all these women blowing us?"

Life on tour with Kiss is a caravan of sixty-three men and women who travel with the band working to achieve a common goal: the evening's concert. People who go out on the road are an interesting lot. They hail from San Francisco and small towns in Kansas, and range in age from fresh-faced twentysomethings to divorced dads in their forties. Many started in local theaters with local bands, and now they are a team working together to transform an empty, 12,500-seat venue into an artist's personal concert hall.

"I don't know how they do it," lead singer Paul Stanley says about the crew. "By the time we go from our dressing rooms to the van, they're already taking the stage down."

## Techs and Roadies

For years, the guys who set up for bands were known as "roadies," but as instruments have evolved, so has the skill level. Today's crew members are commonly referred to as "techs," since they're technicians. They do programming and repair things, custom work—also known as skilled labor. Roadies are pals of the bands who basically lug stuff and do simple setups.

The trend in touring is toward fewer roadies and more technicians. Roadies are younger, and they tend to evolve into technicians through experience.

"I've been on the road for twenty years," confirms Brian Reed, production/tour manager for James Taylor. "I started working for a local band in the Bay area that did cover tunes in bars, four sets a night. I'd work until 3 A.M. and then get up and go to work as a carpenter at 7 in the morning. I did the carpentry full time, and the 'roadie-ing' a couple nights a week. I took the chance and moved to L.A. when a band from Los Angeles did a gig in San Francisco. I helped out, and they were looking for someone full time."

During the performance, a good tech watches the band to make sure that nothing happens that would interfere with the show, or threaten the band. Minor situations include broken guitar strings (there is always a spare axe at the ready), broken drumheads, fallen mics, stuff thrown from the audience (have a nice trip!), or Perrier spilling into a Marshall amp. Techs also watch out for pyrotechnic screwups, electrical problems, PA failure during the show, or even a fan climbing onstage to party with the band. The band crew are the last ones to set up for the show, after the light techs and sound techs are nearly finished.

"Our best load out on the Rolling Stones was forty-two minutes, and that's the entire truck packed," notes Peter Wiltz, the Rolling Stones' keyboard technician. "Groups like Steely Dan, where I had a grand piano and a Fender Rhoads, forty minutes and you're done. It depends on the venue as well; if it's a long push to where the trucks are, obviously it's going to take a little bit longer."

## Starting Life on the Road

The only way to become a roadie is to just do it.

"No one has ever asked me if I had an education," notes Steve Wood, tour manager for bands like Megadeth. "They don't advertise for it. Initially it's knowing somebody or knowing something special."

"My goal was to be a record producer, so I took record production classes at a community college," explains Peter Wiltz. "I took a class called Synthesizer Techniques, and the guy started playing drum sounds from a synthesizer and I was hooked.

"This knowledge gave me my first chance to go on the road. I was in a rehearsal hall, and the guy in the band after us came in with this brand new keyboard in a box. He wanted to save the factory sound because they have pretty good ones that came with the keyboard, but he needed to put in his own. And I said, 'Well I just happen to have my cassette deck right here,' as I just came from school. I helped him out, and he asked me to be his technician. I ended up leaving on a tour about three weeks after that."

"There's no manual for it," says Tim Rozner, Kiss's tour production manager. "People learn from practical application."

There is no such thing as "roadie school." The only way to learn the business is to watch people who are successful doing something and copy it. That, coupled with a little hard work, can make you successful, too. Watch, listen, ask questions, work as a stagehand, work lights, work as third man on sound crews, develop some skills. Learn how to run a spotlight and instantaneously execute cues for the light man barking out commands in the headphones.

As with any job, you have to have a true passion for the roadie work. You need to start out like Tommy Kotchik, the big, short-haired kid, lugging around a bag full of gear, preaching the gospel of "roadie revolution" for the band Bedford. He has been to just about every single show and helped set up and take down after sets. Tommy has many jobs in the band, including transportation, setting up, and actually helping to produce and fund records on the System Untitled label.

"I was hanging out with Ed from Bedford and I would bug the hell out of him for rides to shows," recalls Tommy. "Then I got to carrying stuff around for him, and after six months of doing that, I was like, 'Hey, I'm the roadie!'"

## Setting Up an Arena

Today, a concert runs with the efficiency of a Broadway show. Once you figure out all the equipment that everybody's using, the only thing that changes is the venue. After a while, any tour should get a little boring, because you've got it down to such a routine that you can do it in less and less time.

Let's assume the stage already exists and no assembly is required. The trucks back right up and unload onto the stage (a nearly perfect load-in). The problem is that there is very little space, lots of gear, road cases for that gear, and a specific order in which it all goes up. Sound is usually first, so the PA starts to go up. Stacking the PA is an art. Bass cabinets at the bottom, horns higher up, and bullets on top. It resembles the building of a pyramid and needs to be a little different in almost every venue. The horns have to be aimed at the various sections of the hall, and cords then need to be hooked from each speaker down to the appropriate amps. While this is going on, the light guys are running their cables and getting the lights "up." Racks of lights go up on towers or are suspended from a truss supported by lifters. Once the lights are in place, the soundboard and lightboard both need to be bulldogged out to the sweet spot in the house (no small task, since those puppies are heavy and very fragile). Snakes are run to the boards, and empty road cases are stowed—literally—wherever they fit.

The band roadies (remember them?) are pulling out the band gear and doing some assembly. They really don't have much access to the stage yet since the light guys are pretty much monopolizing that square footage. Now all this has happened in about one hour or so. By the end of hour two, the lights are aimed and the PA is blowing out any cobwebs. Now the band roadies get to place their gear on the marks laid out by the light guys.

The responsibility for making sure things run smoothly falls on the shoulders of the production manager.

"If they do the proper advance work, things should run pretty smoothly," declares Brian Reed.

How long it takes and how complicated a load-in happens to be depends on the size of the room. Stadiums are easy—they have tons and tons of room. You can drive the equipment trucks right to the back of the stage, then unload the trucks from a ramp right onto the playing area. Stadiums and arenas come equipped with stagehands who are paid pretty well to do most of the unloading. They have a clue, so you can instruct them to, say, "Take these instruments out of the cases and put them over there," while the band tech goes off and does something else.

"We can set up Madonna in half an hour," proudly announces Peter Wiltz. "It takes an hour and a half for the Rolling Stones."

That is, if you're not waiting for a forklift or other piece of essential unloading and setup equipment. If you don't have the tools you need—when you need them—setting up a stage can be a terrible task.

Clubs are the worst. You usually have to deal with the club owners and move chairs and tables out of the way just to get your equipment in there. And usually nightclubs don't supply hands to help you. If you get any help at all, it's usually from the bouncer, and he could care less if he drops your instrument. So then you have to go rent something to do the show, and you've already lost the money that you were going to make.

"At the end of load-in, I always think, 'Why am I here?'" says Bill Boyd, a light tech. "But when everything works, it's the best feeling."

The band hightails it out of the venue in its van. For the road crew, however, the work continues: They have to tear the set down, which is a daunting task. Every steel cable has to be unhitched and recoiled, every speaker hauled onto one of a dozen or more convoy trucks. Load-out is a tense, mad scramble that usually takes half the time of the setup.

## Making a Career of It

Making a living by touring always seems like a tenuous existence at best. You have long periods when you're working, and then there's downtime. Will you get another tour? You keep doing it, then somewhere along the line you realize, This is good; I can make a real career out of this.

"I was going to be a musician," laughs Peter Wiltz. "I was going to be drumming—I drummed all through school. Ringo was my idol. I made the transition from above the line to below the line when I went on my first tour. I went into the rehearsal hall as a musician and I came out as a technician. I needed the money. It was more money than I was getting for playing."

As a musician, you might make $25 per man at a party. The position of technician/roadie/tour manager starts at $350 a week, expenses covered, and grows from there.

"It was 1987 when I last worked as a carpenter and realized that I really don't like that as much as going on the road," recalls Brian Reed. "I told myself, 'You can't fall back on going into carpentry between tours,' because it was keeping me from concentrating on what I really like. That's when I really did this full-time. It's always been a pretty decent living."

## Specialization

In the days of tube amps, going on the road was a drum kit, a couple of Fender amps, and a couple of keyboards. There wasn't a whole lot inside of it. It's like cars. It used to be easy to fix a car; now everything is run off specialized microchips. Life on the road has evolved as well. Once you get beyond schlepping equipment, you begin to specialize in one segment of setting up an arena for the concert. If you're musical, it will be equipment. Like lights? Electricity? Making sure it all flows smoothly? There are dozens of roles that need to be filled when you're putting on a live performance—what you choose depends on your skill set.

"My organizational skills are strong, which is why I enjoy being a production manager more than anything," points out Brian Reed. "As a production manager, you oversee the crew, you advance all the technical details for a show. Usually a production manager is also the stage manager as well, unless it's a really big show. You oversee the load-in and load-out, keep things running on time. Take care of the travel and the hotel and the per diems for the crew. I like it mainly because that's what I'm good at. To be a keyboard tech, you need to know MIDI and you need to know computers, and my mind just doesn't work very well when it comes to that stuff, so I just gravitated toward what works."

## Tour Production

If you're in tour production, you're working on the tour months before it begins.

"You try to book the dates as far in advance as possible to get the proper routing, so you're not doing a zigzag all over the country," advises Brian. "You want to keep the drives as short as possible. Ideally that can be a year in advance, but that isn't always the case."

You need to organize your stagehands, figure out the time you need to start loading in, arrange for the power, the security, where the trucks are going to unload, and the catering. You need to make sure you get all the backstage phone numbers at the venues in advance, so you can list them in the itinerary, as well as directions to the venue.

"If you speak to the promoter enough and get your faxes going, you walk in knowing that you've done a good advance. So there's really no reason why things should go wrong—but things do," chuckles Brian.

## The Tour Manager

When you've seen it all, you're ready to be a tour manager.

"I've been around the world countless times, met everybody, done everything," declares Steve Wood, who has tour-managed Kiss, Soundgarden, Megadeth, and Peter Frampton.

"The key to keeping a job is versatility and blending with the employers," he advises. "Like being able to understand what their needs are and not having to ask them every step of the way. You have to be able to take lots of initiative and you have to be able to wear lots of different hats. You have to do more than one thing at one time and you have to blend in with your surroundings and the people you're with. You're with them the whole time, so they have to like you as a person."

You have to have a rapport with the act because you're their tour manager. You're personally involved with everything that they do, including their family—you have to find babysitters for wives and girlfriends—you're privy to a lot of personal relations.

"The most important thing in the relationship between an artist and a tour manager is trust," notes Chris Cornell, former Soundgarden frontman and current solo artist. "An artist is relying on you to help them do their job."

# Techs

Techs are often former audiovisual geeks or musicians who have stepped out of the spotlight. Drum techs tend to be ex-drummers or aspiring drummers (or, sometimes, really bad drummers). Ditto for keyboard techs, guitar techs, violin techs, and even hammer dulcimer techs. They want to be near the music. Playing with instruments gives them a rush.

A tech's responsibilities include the setup and maintenance of the instrument or instruments he is assigned, running to local music stores for guitar picks and strings, tuning guitars, keeping the musicians furnished with water or a Heineken or freshly squeezed carrot juice during the show, and, most important, watching.

Techs are folks who take care of the equipment. To be a keyboard technician, you need to know MIDI. MIDI is a technology that lets your computer speak a musical language. It started in 1983. With a MIDI card, your computer can talk to your synthesizer, you can change the sound coming from the computer, and you see all the parameters on one screen.

"Without MIDI, you're looking at this little tiny screen on the keyboard, and you have to press buttons and go page by page by page to find all these parameters," explains Peter Wiltz. "With MIDI, it's all on one screen on the computer, and I can just click to a certain cell and change the value and it will change the sound."

There are 16 MIDI channels and about 127 controllers that are used to program the computer to do anything you need it to do. Each machine has its own personality—one machine may not be able to do what another machine does, in which case you'll need both. MIDI language lets them speak to each other. You can also use sequencers. Sequencers can record MIDI data and performances. Today people are using a lot of sequencing and a lot of sampling.

You can't get away from MIDI; it's even infiltrated guitars, with all the effects pedals triggering MIDI devices. Push a button and it will change your program from echo to reverb or echo to crunch. MIDI has become standard equipment because it works.

# Getting Lucky

A key part of moving up in this business is getting lucky. You hear about a situation—like the time the Rolling Stones' keyboard tech passed away—and you go after it, the way Peter Wiltz did.

"The Rolling Stones were in the recording studio in Los Angeles. Don Was was producing, and the recording engineer was Ed Cherney. I had built some effects racks for Ed Cherney, and he called me when the Rolling Stones needed some road cases. We built three cases, two for

Charlie Watts and one for Pierre the guitar tech. When I was down there, I said, 'I read that your keyboard technician passed away. If you guys need someone for the tour after this album, I'd be very interested in helping you out.' And they said, 'Oh yeah, sure . . . sure, right. We've got 150,000 people that want the job, but the least you can do is send over a résumé.' So, I faxed over my résumé. About two months later, the Rolling Stones are done with their record, they're leaving Los Angeles, they're packing up their stuff, and I get a phone call from Pierre, the guitar technician, saying, 'Didn't we buy this piano case from you guys?'

"And I said, 'Yeah.'

"And he said, 'It doesn't fit.'

"'I'll be down, right now.' So I went back to the studio, and I brought my notes and tried to make it fit. The case company had missed by an inch on one of the measurements. So we made a whole other case for these guys. I said, 'I'll eat it.' And Pierre says, 'Don't I have your résumé as a keyboard technician?'

"I said, 'Yeah, you'd better.'

"Then I don't hear from him for another few days, and one evening I get a call from Dave, who's Mick's guitar tech, and Pierre, and they're out together. And they said, 'What are you doing?' And I said, 'I'm in a little blues club on Ventura Boulevard,' and they said, 'Stay right there, we're coming down.'

"They came down and we were watching some blues people play. And they said, 'Do you play any music?' And I said, 'Do I play music? Yeah, I play a little bit of keyboards and a bunch of drums, and I have a rehearsal studio in my warehouse.'

"That night, we played music until three o'clock in the morning. We were just jamming, and that was my audition. They didn't care that I was a keyboard technician all that much. They just wanted somebody to be in their crew band."

## Salaries

"I have a huge bank account," laughs Peter Wiltz.

Just as there is no handbook, there is also no union. All fees are negotiable. Salaries can range from $35,000 to more than $150,000 per tour—but those are sixteen- to eighteen-hour days, and no overtime. The band does pay for the crew's meals, but usually not its insurance.

"There are a lot of upsides to this job," Brian Reed observes. "You get to have a lot of fun; it's a very relaxed atmosphere as there's no real dress code. When a tour is running along smoothly, and you've got the routine down, it feels like summer camp. There's a lot of kidding around: You can get the job done and still have a lot of fun."

"You go with what pays your bills," shrugs stagehand Scott Nordvold. "And this is steady work. I know what I'll be doing for the next sixteen months."

## Free Time

One of the downsides of being on the road is this: You don't always get a lot of free time, since it can cost a band upwards of $100,000 a day to keep its crew on the road. How much time off you get depends on the tour, how long the drive is to the next city, and what time you get there. Sometimes all you do is get out of the bus and go into the arena—maybe go for a run in the afternoon. That might be all you get to see of the city.

There are so many long hours on the job that it's pretty easy to neglect the rest of your life.

## Girls, Girls, Girls

You think of life on the road as full of girls, girls, girls, and sometimes that's the case. On the road with Kiss, picking up chicks is made easier by "pussy passes"—laminates that allow access to all backstage areas except Kiss's dressing rooms.

"Maybe you get a lot of girls if you want them," notes Peter Wiltz. Male crew members admit that "the girls" are a big reason they subject themselves to such a grueling job, and the girls can be many. One-night stands are fairly easy to come by. But try having a relationship on the road, and see what happens.

"Sometimes it's hard even starting a relationship. You're not around or you might only be around for a short time and you can't just meet somebody when you want to," admits Brian. "Just because I'm getting home from the road for a couple months doesn't mean I'm going to meet somebody right then. I could meet somebody just before I leave and that usually falls apart. Or you try and work a relationship where you're gone a lot, and the woman decides she doesn't want that. You fall into the trap of thinking you can have a long-distance relationship, and they just don't work."

## The Ups and the Downs

There are upsides and downsides to going on the road for years on end. The benefits are you get to travel and stay in semi-fancy hotels and hang around rock stars. And your bank account grows. The downsides are you're away from home for weeks and months at a time and if you have any personal relationship, or life relationship, forget it, because it's over. Most techs say their wives leave them, take their children and their paychecks, and vamoose.

"You give up a life to have a career," concludes Peter.

# BAND MANAGEMENT:
## *Won't Get Fooled Again*

> We had done as much work as we could in New England on our own. We were selling out everywhere, getting unbelievable radio play and we were selling 1,000 records a week. But it was all going to fizzle away unless we got help. Our manager brought Godsmack up to a whole new level.
>
> —SULLY ERNA
> GODSMACK
> REPUBLIC RECORDS

*G*ood managers are like good parents. They take care of the band, nurture them, look out for their best interests. They're the ones who support the band through the roller coaster of making an album. They will see that the band gets to the gig on time when the bus breaks down, and deny to the media that a member was arrested for having sex with a minor.

JJ French has had platinum success as manager and producer for Sevendust. The union came together quite simply. JJ had a reputation. When Sevendust wanted to tour New York City, they asked JJ to book them some gigs. So he got them into places like the famed folk club the Bitter End. TVT Records (Trent Reznor's old label) signed them in June 1996, and they were on their way. Their self-titled debut album has already gone gold.

"Somebody came up to me while I was standing on the side of the stage watching Sevendust perform and said, 'Wow, I was watching your expression and you looked like a proud parent.' And I thought, You know, I am," offers JJ. "We had a following of 300 people four years ago, and we ended up with a following of 400,000. That was satisfying."

He asserts that a good manager needs to understand the music business and know how to deal with the extraordinary obstacles any band confronts.

"Within Twisted Sister's history, I've experienced attempted murders among band members. In the early days of the band there was a gun drawn on another band member," recalls JJ. "One guy got hit by a car; one guy lost an eye to cancer; another guy died of a brain tumor. I've had my truck stolen and held for ransom. I've had my trucks blown up. I've had equipment lost on highways. I've had band members OD and choke in front of record company executives and blow record deals. How much more can I say? Drug overdoses, alcohol abuse. If a manager goes through that stuff and is still standing, he can deal with it."

## A Manager's Responsibilities

"Management is pretty much a thankless job," declares Bob Chiappardi, former manager and current president and CEO of Concrete Marketing. "If something goes wrong, you're to blame; if something goes right, it's because the artist is so wonderful. It really has nothing to do with you. So, you lose no matter what. It really is hard. When something goes wrong, the band goes to the manager and piss and moan because their girlfriends didn't get the right backstage pass."

Although you're in the center of the fabulous world of rock 'n' roll, managers are much more administrative—they're not creative. The manager both oversees and performs different kinds of services for a band. Depending on the service package the band and the manager agree on, management responsibilities most commonly include:

- Band promotion and media management.
- Tour and show bookings: Scheduling of band performances and helping the band to determine their current market value; budgeting of food, lodging, and travel expenses while the band is on the road.
- Production consultation and management: Overseeing and performing sound and light engineering, stage setup, set scheduling, and prep work for the event.
- Contract Work: Writing and keeping on file performance agreements, technical riders, and hospitality riders.
- Press kits: Compiling information the media will need, including written bios, photos of the band, and media clippings.

- Video press kits: Arranging for the production of a live-performance video that's professionally edited and arranged.
- Web space, mailbox, and dial-in: Overseeing and performing Web site design, maintenance, and updating of shows and band information on the site.
- MP3 site: Hosting, encoding, and maintaining a half-page space, including a thirty-second audio clip, for preview before purchase.
- Creative consultation: Helping to or hiring a professional graphic designer to design the look of the CD.
- CD distribution: Overlooking expenses for and facilitating studio time, CD packaging, and distribution. (Management with good connections can offer their bands discounted recording studio time and can have CDs pressed and packaged for as low as $1,335 for 1,000 CDs.)

Managers are also expected to maintain an ongoing dialogue with record labels, and keep them focused on marketing and promoting the acts.

"With the label, I'm a cheerleader for the band," declares David Krebs. "You've got to be reasonably optimistic without being the one that overhypes. A lot of elements have to be measured—each band is different—but you've got to play up the band's strengths and minimize their weaknesses."

## Where Experience Counts

Like a diplomat, a manager has to anticipate problems and troubleshoot any issues or controversies that arise. As a manager, you have to know how to talk to people—whether it be road crews, labels, promoters, or merchandise people. Singer/songwriter Sammy Hagar claims that he would still be in Van Halen and the band would still be one of the biggest in the world if the group's manager, Ed Leffler, hadn't passed away.

"If Ed Leffler were still alive and I was still in the band, nothing would have changed—we'd still be the biggest band in the world. All it takes is confidence and you do the right thing," insists Sammy Hagar. "I learned a lot from Ed—he managed me for eighteen years. Now I just apply what he taught me—the consciousness of 'Hey, you don't do it for money.' That's the way he approached it. First you've got to want to do the gig and it's got to be the right thing to do."

A good manager brings to the position both wisdom and people skills. The manager engages in many conversations on lots of different levels. As the liaison between the commerce of the record and the creative side of the musician, a manager has to explain each one to the other because artists and businesspeople live in totally different worlds. A good manager is someone who understands both sides and interprets both sides' needs, among many other talents.

"Managers are like coaches. They make sure that all the elements are working as close to 100 percent as possible—from the record company to the public relations company, to the agent, to the band's crew, to the band. It's a manager's job to make sure it's all together," notes David Krebs, president of the band management firm Krebs Communications.

"Being a manager is about relationships," confirms James Citkovic of Countdown Entertainment. "Say you get the artist a movie deal. There will always be someone coming up from behind who is ready to try and take over, and tell the artist he can do better."

Leverage is key once a band is signed. Managers who don't have leverage get trampled by record companies. A head of marketing will stick a fork in a manager's long-term desires to tour or make an expensive video, and if the band doesn't have a manager who's willing to fight hard on their behalf, the head of marketing will prevail. The group gets shoved under the rug in a heartbeat, unless they've got someone to pull for them. If you choose to manage a band, this responsibility will fall on your shoulders. A band's success will be all about who you are and what you can do for the band.

"Van Halen's manager Ed Leffler used lines like, 'If you're never in, you're never out,'" recalls Sammy Hagar. "He'd say things like, 'You don't want to be on the cover of *Time* magazine because once you're on the cover of *Time* magazine, you're too fashionable and then you're out when that fashion passes.' When he managed us, Van Halen was never fashionable. People wrote us off—but we were selling 6–7 million records at any given time—we were selling out any arena in the world. He was so damn right. Here I am still cruising right along through the trends, and I've never been in, so I'm never out."

You'll know if you're a good manager. Either people will return your phone calls, or they won't. Either your clients will like you or they won't. Either you will have your team well enough organized to pull off a headlining performance—or you won't.

> **Commit it to memory:** *The music business is all about leverage; it's all about who you know. A big key to success is good relationships.*

## Ways to Get into Management

If you don't have twenty-five years of experience and still want to get into management, manage an unknown band. You'll get the experience you need, but be aware of the pitfalls. Once an unknown band gets a record deal, they're usually convinced to sign with a management firm that has more clout.

Lots of bands have friends as their managers—the roadies-turned-reps who do everything, are there to help out, and have all the best intentions. Any knucklehead can be a manager, but friends without connections rarely cut it after a major label comes along and offers a deal. But sometimes a buddy-turned-manager makes a great tour manager, and can take care of the band on the road once the group breaks into the big leagues.

"A manager is wrong if he has no understanding of how the industry works, or if he does not know anything about your style of music," observes Nancy Camp of Drastic Measures, Inc.

Steve Stewart, manager of Stone Temple Pilots, was as green as grass when the group first got signed, but he learned. Steve was a hard worker and a good learner, and he remained Stone Temple Pilots' manager through three multiplatinum records.

Or, you may be fortunate enough to hook up with some veteran elder statesman who's got twenty-five years' experience in the music business and might be willing to take you under his wing—someone like Miles Copeland, the CEO of ARK 21 Records. As a kid in the seventies, he created his first record label, I.R.S. Records, because nobody would sign his brother's band, the Police. His motivation: "I just thought, 'I hate somebody telling me *no.*'" Now, Miles takes pleasure in developing a strong stable of talent—both above and below the line.

"I love working with other managers who are new, and helping them," Miles declares. "Now that the record companies have gotten so huge, they can't take the time to think about an artist's long-term career."

## Love Your Bands

You have to look at the musical acts as a business, but you'll never be a great manager if you don't love what you're doing. You've really got to be into the music you're working with—live it and breathe it—if you're going to help a band succeed.

"It's hard to manage if you're not into the music," says David Krebs. "Management is not like a label, where you have to satisfy all sorts of tastes. I have to satisfy my tastes in order to get motivated."

> **Commit it to memory:** *Surround yourself with music you really care about.*

More than music is needed for good band-management relationships. With twenty-five years of music experience behind him, Miles chooses to work with bands who require a minimal investment. He admits: "I operate risk averse. I won't come in and line somebody's pockets. I say, 'Look, if you're prepared to play ball here, let's work together to create something for you. But you've got to record at a reasonable price, you've got to go out there and work.'" If an act isn't fighting there right alongside you, it's just not worth it.

"I'd rather put my money into promotion than put my money into the group buying themselves cars and lining their pockets. There'll be time for that if they succeed."

## The Role of Management

The role of a manager changes as the band's career evolves. When a band is in its grassroots phase, there's nothing a manager can do that artists can't simply do themselves. A manager will put together a press kit; contact the media; send out press releases; cultivate relationships with radio, the print press, and retail; and, if you're lucky, get a group gigs. A band can build a name for itself on their own. It's once they've built a name for themselves that they need someone to help take them further. A manager derives satisfaction from taking a band to the next level.

"We had done as much work as we could in New England on our own," recalls Sully Erna of the band Godsmack. Godsmack had established themselves in a regional market—they were selling out shows, getting heavy local radio airplay, and selling a thousand records a week. "If we didn't get help and step up to getting a good attorney, a good manager, and a good record label, we were going to be one of the bands who were—'Oh, what happened to them?' We signed a management deal with Paul Geary, and he took us national."

Godsmack broke on their first album, as did Sevendust, but they're both lucky. There's no hard and fast rule as to how much time and money you invest in a band to make it pay off.

"Everything is different," reflects JJ French. "Twisted Sister spent a lot of time, effort, perseverance, and thousands and thousands and thousands of dollars over ten years trying to get a record deal. Sevendust got a deal within eight months of my getting involved, and the demo cost $350. That's the difference. There's the high and the low of the business."

When wooing your bands, don't create unrealistic expectations. The out-of-the-box success of groups like Godsmack and Sevendust are still a relatively rare occurrence. Work to make a band the top draw in their market: If you create the buzz, the deals will come.

"The biggest problem for most managers is promising too much," says Keith Abbott, president of Abbott Promotions. "Some of them get so wrapped up in making money that they tend to forget their client's needs and wants. It's that whole *Jerry McGuire* thing. I think the best managers are those who put the music first and the money second.

## Management's Role after Signing

"You have to be able to convince somebody at the label that they're smart enough to make the deal," explains David Krebs. "Getting a band signed takes a lot of sending around tapes and showcasing. Then you sign with the label you think is best for the group. In deciding this, you try to balance who's most passionate about a band, and what the label roster looks like. There are too many intangibles—it's all guesswork."

Once a band has a record deal, the manager is a necessary voice inside the record company to keep the label on its toes. Remember that a big record label may be working two dozen other acts in addition to your own band. As a manager, you need to be strong to keep the label focused on your act.

Your band is what is of the utmost importance to you, not the other twenty acts that are going for radio that week. As a manager, you should be getting your band's name out there to the right people as often as you possibly can.

"If an act has a good manager, it makes my job a lot easier," explains Kathy Callahan, senior director of western regional sales at Windham Hill Records. "I like a manager who knows what he wants the artist to do and has a vision about where the artist is going. The manager should be the visionary who can do that for the record company. He decides how often the artist should go on tour. There are positives and negatives to management from a record label's point of view. The manager can be your best friend or your worst enemy."

A connected manager offers bands the best of all possible worlds. Steve Stewart Management will gain exposure for one of its emerging bands, like 12 Volt Sex, by putting them on the bill with a more established act like Loudmouth. Or, if Stewart were to feel that a band like Sonichrome might better work out on tour with Semisonic, he could, in return, offer Semisonic a couple of dates on the Stone Temple Pilots tour.

Management is all about leveraging your assets, and making the most of the situation. A manager needs to be strong, decisive, firm, and together. Management is the foundation of the business side of the band. When management is unstable, it leads to band disharmony and interrupted careers.

## How Much Do Managers Make?

Managers are not employees of a band; rather, they are business partners. The right manager does not work for a salary—he gets a percentage of receipts only.

"Managers should never ever charge the artist a salary," notes Jean Segendorph, a partner in PolySutra Entertainment, a modern rock firm based in New York City. "You pay a percentage on what comes in."

A manager normally takes 10–20 percent of a group's gross earnings right off the top. The exact number will vary from act to act and will depend on the type of responsibilities you are performing for the act.

"Your percentage really depends on what you negotiate, what you're doing, how many acts you have, how big your staff is," notes JJ French. "Management is a 'We want you' type of business. What are you willing to give up in order to get somebody? It works both ways—wanting can emanate from either the band or the manager."

As a good manager, you deserve whatever you've earned. Early on, you had to stand by your bands. Back then, they probably had nothing but good music to attract you. Throughout their evolution, you put up with a lot of trash and have taken on a lot of responsibility, and you don't get to do the fun stuff like playing on stage.

One of the benefits of being a manager is that you can draw income from a variety of different sources—you get your management commission, you get your touring commission, you get record royalties, you get a publishing commission—as a manager, you get a commission on whatever a band makes money on. Is that ample motivation?

As their business manager, you may want to give the record and publishing company a letter of direction of payment. This letter, usually written by the manager and signed by the group, indicates that the artist has directed the record label to pay specific members of the team, like the manager, lawyer, and so on, directly out of that check. A letter of direction to the record label might say: "When you're getting ready to write that check for $100,000 to our act, instead of writing $100,000 to the artist, write $85,000 to the artist and $15,000 to me, subject to the artist's approval."

## Keys to Success

One of the keys to success in management is keeping expenses down. Another is identifying your audience. Another is personality.

Keeping expenses down is easy. You don't need a big, flashy office; you just need a bunch of people gathering and disseminating information by telephone and computer. That objective can be accomplished in a variety of ways besides having an office on Sunset Boulevard.

"My overhead is low. I'm in survival mode," declares Miles Copeland about how he's running ARK 21. "I will be here five years from now."

Miles works with artists he enjoys and who are fun to work with. His experience allows him to go beyond the traditional methods of marketing and promoting bands. Whether through movies or by stickers, Miles is interested in promoting his artists in a myriad of ways.

"I'm very interested in developing parts of the record business that I think have not been totally glutted by the majors," he admits. "I'm always looking for the niche market."

Again, one of the most important characteristics a manager needs is people skills—the ability to make deals gracefully and make all parties feel pleased and satisfied. Businesspeople tend to be rather straightforward, but "you have to balance what the artists want to do with what they need to do," according to Miles. "When it's out of balance, when an artist never wants to make the concessions that are necessary, you're out of balance."

Management is all about give-and-take, yin and yang, and the positive interaction of events to achieve the goals set for the band.

# BOOKING AND PROMOTION:

## *Rock 'N' Roll All Night* ‖:

There's a simple logistic in tour promotion that everybody needs to understand—there are more bands than venues.

—VINCE REESE, PRESIDENT
SASQUATCH ENTERTAINMENT

*W*elcome to the $1.3 billion live-music industry. If you succeed, you can make a lot of money in this area. For example, in 1998, the year's top-grossing tour ($89.3 million) was that of the Rolling Stones, who sold 1.5 million tickets in North America and managed to pull in $10.8 million for a single four-night booking at Oakland Stadium.

Sounds nice, doesn't it? Wouldn't we all like to work with bands like the Stones? Be advised, however: Booking venues for young start-up bands is an exacting art—plan wrong and you lose your profits. Whether you are the agent working with the band to get the gig or the concert promoter for the venue, you need to have a concrete promotional strategy in place to ensure that everything goes smoothly and the event is a success. All elements must be in alignment—the venue, the audience, the drive to the next gig, marketing and promotion for the gig, and the beat goes on. How you go about booking a venue in a particular town is another process. It's very territorial and it's divided up geographically. In every city there are people with established reputations of either doing it right or doing it wrong.

Let's keep the math simple, real, and small-scale. Let's say rising stars Ben Folds Five sold out the Club Caprice, in Redondo Beach, California, on November 29. That's five hundred tickets at $15 each, for a box office gross of $7,500. Let's say the band's take was a modest $5,000. The agent then gets 15 percent of that, which is $750. Multiply that by a hundred dates and that's $75,000, the profit for a moderately successful tour. If the agent is working five bands at once, she makes a $400,000 profit. (On the other hand, the five band members walk away with just $15,000 apiece.)

Take an arena band—say, Fleetwood Mac, who grossed $1,620,725 for two nights at Great Woods. The mighty Mac pockets the door, and the booking agent gets 15 percent of the total profits (including concessions, parking fees, and merchandising), which totals a little more than $243,000. A mere ten engagements on that scale puts nearly $2.5 million in some lucky agent's pocket.

The concert promoter, who is in charge of promoting the event for the venue, traditionally has made his money from the profits that remain after the artists' fees, agent fee, advertising, production, and other costs have been paid out of the concert's gross. But there's been a paradigm shift in the major-concert business over the past decade. Superstar artists have been able to command a growing portion of the box-office receipts, leaving promoters to rely on things like concession sales, parking fees, merchandising (T-shirt and souvenir sales), and other revenue streams for their profits.

Sure, it takes a lot of knowledge and patience to be a good booking agent or concert promoter. It's a tough job, but the potential profits are huge.

"Booking a good tour is all about having good relationships with the people who work in the venues," notes Mike Luba of Madison House Tour Promotions in Denver. "They know that if you call them and say, 'Hey, this is the real deal,' you're going to send them the real deal."

There are certain places all over the country where people know if they go to that venue, they're going to hear good music.

"The feeling of the room and the venue is critical to the overall experience," Mike Luba points out. "It's really critical to have access to the right rooms for your band when they're just starting out. That access comes from years of doing it. People also need to know that when you call them, you're going to be straight with them."

The Fillmore in San Francisco is one of those places that can do miracles for a band's reputation. When the rock concert industry was evolving in the sixties, the typical promoter was a hippie entrepreneur, producing shows out of a love for music and the drive to make a little cash. A few were artist/impresarios like San Francisco's Bill Graham, a brass-knuckled businessman who turned the process of presenting a concert into a performance in itself. He sweated details—like greeting the crowd outside, monitoring sound equipment quality, tutoring his staff on conduct—to make sure the overall experience of attending a show was a good one. Graham himself was one of the legendary Fillmore's most interesting attractions.

Graham was midwife to the psychedelic San Francisco scene, nurturing such groundbreaking outfits as Jefferson Airplane and the Grateful Dead. As the gatekeeper of two of only a handful of rock ballrooms in the nation in the late sixties and early seventies, he played key roles in supporting such bands as The Who, the Jimi Hendrix Experience, Big Brother and the Holding Company, Janis Joplin, The Band, Bob Dylan, the J. Geils Band, the Allman Brothers Band, and the Rolling Stones.

These days, in any given week there are seventy-five bands clamoring to play the Fillmore. A half-dozen of these appeals will be in the form of references, tapes from managers, agents, and friends of bands swearing, "This is the real deal." Another few will be rebookings—bands that have been okayed to play there, but have yet to work it into their touring schedule. Then there will be tapes from bands that have already played there.

"When I booked the Deli Creeps in there, I was contacted by the Fillmore," notes Vince Reese of Sasquatch Entertainment. "They don't take unsolicited material."

Only one tour package is going to get the shot, and that depends on who can do the business. Who can sell the most tickets? Who can get additional revenues for parking, beer, merchandising (the Fillmore takes 35 percent)? Even though it's music, it's still business. Who can make the best profits?

## Booking a Venue

"I'll give almost any band a chance," declares Vince Reese. "If a band is good, I'll give them a Wednesday or a Thursday night as a starter. For a San Francisco nightclub, I usually ask that they guarantee about twenty-five people per band. If they can bring in that many people, I'll book them a show for a weekend. If they can't bring in that many people, I try them again one other time, and then if they can't do it I have to let them go."

Once a band is selected to play a venue, it's business as usual. Each venue has a fairly standard procedure for all its events. It is the job of the agent and the promoter to make sure each step runs smoothly for every date of the tour. Typically, an event will go something like this:

1. The venue contacts the artists' agent and presents an offer to the agent on the selected act
2. Details are negotiated

3. Contracts are signed, deposit checks are sent, rider requirements are negotiated
4. The agent sends the venue all promotional materials
5. All sound, light, and backline requirements are ordered
6. Professional stagehands are arranged for
7. A time schedule for the day of the event is made
8. All hospitality is arranged for
9. The promoter arrives at the venue site before the production gear and crew
10. The promoter coordinates the load-in of all equipment and backline
11. The promoter sets out hospitality for the crew and artist
12. The promoter oversees sound check
13. The promoter sets out meals for the crew and artists
14. Final payments to the production staff and artist are made
15. The promoter coordinates the load-out of all equipment

# Making a Tour Profitable

A profitable tour is a perfect balance of many elements—venue, band, audience taste. To make a tour profitable without label tour support means everything has to be right. Look at it this way: If a band's sole goal is to be profitable, they could be a cover band and go out and make tremendous amounts of money playing corporate gigs and weddings and events.

"A lot of it has to be a willingness on the band's part to almost eat it up front. They cannot make decisions based on money but based on what's right for their career," confirms Mike Luba.

Bands that are trying to establish long-term music careers outside the constraints of corporate music always strive to be headliners.

"When we were first building the band Galactic, we would walk away from money that we really needed to play gigs because it would either be to open up for someone, or it would put us in front of a lot of people," notes Mike. "The whole premise was to let the band headline so people could actually experience the band."

"Our fans have grown with us from the beginning," confirms Scott Stapp, lead vocalist for the triple-platinum band Creed. "We'd play a city and there would be 40 people there. The next time there would be 150, and the next time there would be 500—it was all a word of mouth thing. They'd say, 'You need to go see Creed. They put on a really good show.'"

The philosophy among the current generation of bands is: Never open if you can avoid it. It's much better to play for a hundred fans of your own than to go out and play for a thousand people who are there to see someone else. That way, people actually come for the experience and you're not treated as a sidenote. You have to make sure your music is taken seriously.

Today's audience takes an active part in the promotion of a band. The group is about more than just music; it's about lifestyle, developing the "Kiss Army," so to speak. Fans talk the band up—promoting the band via word of mouth.

> **Commit it to memory:** *Fifty percent of us try something new not because of advertising, but because someone told us about it.*

"If the band is good, there are going to be people who are going to take them under their wings, and the trick is connecting all those dots," notes Mike. "Then when the bands go out, they have friends and family in every city."

There are things you can do to support a band when they go out on the road, so it's not just a bunch of guys in a band or on a bus driving around the country. Make sure all the print and electronic media know what's going on, and that the radio stations are filled in and offered interviews. There should be someone out there in every town hanging up flyers and posters.

Concrete Marketing has a street team. The team goes out and promotes their shows in exchange for cool perks, like tickets for shows, advance tapes, promo stuff, and the like. The duties of the street team include:

- Handing out flyers and posters at record stores, skate shops, clothing stores, etc.
- Handing out flyers at local shows
- Informing the promoter about any local fanzines or music papers
- Spreading the word on Internet newsgroups, music folders, etc.
- Checking to see if a CD is in stock at local record shops

Booking a good tour really has to do with long-term relationships with the promoters. The promoters know their market the best. Draw on their experience about when is a good time to come to town, so that you don't exceed what the market will bear at any given moment.

It's a rough road and not all promoters can manage it.

"A lot of smaller promoters have become part of larger companies," says Gary Bongiovanni, editor-in-chief of the live-concert industry bible *Pollstar.* "The capital threshold that's required to compete in the industry today is immense."

## Agents and Concerts

An agent has only one function: getting a band work.

"The whole trick to it is there is a finite amount of spaces for the music to be made and there's an infinite number of bands out there all battling for the same shot at the same venues," summarizes Mike Luba.

Everyone carves out his or her niche. The Marquee Group has a small but powerful booking company that handles Billy Joel, Luther Vandross, and the entire Q-Prime Management roster, which includes Madonna, Metallica, and Courtney Love. The Marquee Group is also a leader in developing corporate sponsorship for arenas. Last year it reportedly brokered a $100-million-plus, twenty-year deal with the Staples retail chain that allows the office products company to place its name on the new sports arena in Los Angeles.

Big business likes to do business with big business. When an agent is booking a tour, she'll find that there are some monster businesses like SFX that handle all major venues all over the country. Then there are some folks who concentrate on regional business, and others who focus only on their local venues.

For example, in the northeastern United States, Don Law's Tea Party Concerts promotes shows in more than a dozen major venues from Providence, Rhode Island, to Augusta, Maine, including the FleetCenter, Great Woods, the Worcester Centrum, the Worcester Auditorium, the Providence Civic Center, and Harborlights Pavilion. Tea Party Concerts also books five Boston clubs and has ownership interests in many of those venues.

When you get into concert promotion, you'll find yourself working with everyone from kids who just graduated from college all the way up to people like Bill Graham and John Scher, who have thirty-five years of experience. It's all about who's in charge of booking talent for any given club, and about how many people they can draw.

"Sure, I can book a band," declares Vince Reese, "but the band is the one who has to make sure that they draw fans. When I was doing the booking and I wanted my friends to go, I'd say, 'Oh, we're doing a barbecue afterwards' . . . and the bands need to put more gumption in it too. . . . A lot of bands just don't put the energy into bringing in the audience. They want other people to do it."

## SFX

The end of the millennium saw a big change in the concert industry. Major corporate conglomerate SFX went on a half-billion-dollar spending spree, buying up all the independent promoters, and becoming the first nationwide concert promoter. That brings a staggering end to a thirty-year history of booking agents haggling with a series of regional promoters throughout the United States to arrange such tours, and to those agents and promoters getting their piece of the pie.

"The alternative is to try to do it on your own, and we saw what happened when Pearl Jam did that," says E. J. Devonale of Hard Head Management.

Indeed, Pearl Jam's 1995 tour has become emblematic of what happens when a strong-willed, music-biz giant gets crossed. The Seattle group's attempt to avoid places affiliated with TicketMaster—to liberate their fans from the tyranny of high service fees—proved so disastrous that it threatened to destroy the band. Pearl Jam's exhausting tour through off-the-path sites resulted in cancellations, unfilled houses, bad production, and the eventual collapse of singer Eddie Vedder from the heat of the battle.

SFX is making touring a one-stop event by rampantly purchasing venues. In 1998, SFX went on a carefully orchestrated buying spree, spending $449 million on seven companies. The largest purchase was Houston's PACE Entertainment, for $130 million. SFX paid $65 million for the San Francisco–based promoting firm of Bill Graham Presents. It also acquired New York's Delsener/Slater; Fisher, Indiana's Sunshine Promotions; Atlanta's Concert/Southern Promotions; and St. Louis's Contemporary Group. And SFX bought the research/publishing/promotions company SJS Entertainment/Network Magazine Group in Los Angeles.

"When I got out of college, I worked at a monster concert company on the East Coast, and I learned how *not* to do everything," observes Mike Luba. "I learned a lot of the skeavy, real terrible parts of the music business, where the musicians and the artists are treated like widgets. The musicians have nothing to do with it: A concert is about selling beer and parking tickets and how much money you can make. It's like corporate anything. The thing that's really disappointing is that these companies were all started by people who loved music and they become so tainted after a while."

The man behind SFX Entertainment is power broker Robert Sillerman, an entertainment-biz wizard who amassed a fortune's worth of radio stations, sold them off last year, and then began systematically buying up a half-dozen of the country's best-run, most powerful independent concert-promotion companies. Now SFX controls a national web of forty-two major concert venues and more than a hundred clubs and small theaters.

SFX dominates the concert market. With venues ranging from the 25,000-capacity Meadows Amphitheater in Connecticut to the Portland Opera House, it can keep nearly three hundred bands a night working throughout the country and book a major national tour for a star as big as the Backstreet Boys with a single phone call. One call to a manager, and SFX could cut out regional promoters and deny them the commissions of 10–15 percent or better that booking agencies deduct from artists' fees. It's one-stop shopping, with a cash bonus for artists and their managers.

"The fewer people who make money off a tour, the better it is for the artist," explains Janet Billig, who represents the Breeders, Lisa Loeb, Cibo Matto, and the Lemonheads, and has also worked with Nirvana. "Fewer cooks in the kitchen makes for an easier tour. The more people involved, the more diluted the artist's directions about how a concert should be promoted, advertised, and presented—their more specific needs and requests—become. Everything gets further diluted with each level of people involved."

With SFX running the concert business, you can also expect more in the way of corporate sponsorship and corporate block-seating purchases, meaning the cheap seats may be all that's left for the consumer.

"We certainly think there's something to be learned from the sports business in terms of taking advantage of those opportunities," notes Tim Klahs, SFX investor relations director. "There's somewhat of a time lag between the music business and the sports business in terms of the corporate world using these venues for sponsorships," he says. "I believe we'll see the gap between the two closing."

## Getting into Promotion

People in tour promotion start early. For Vince Reese, it was selling merchandise for Winterland Productions. He went out on tour and sold T-shirts for three years; most other people only last one tour at the same job. He was good, so they moved him up.

Mike Luba started with Cellar Door Productions on the East Coast. He learned the corporate way, then went out and started Madison House Tour Promotions, a more organic company.

"The String Cheese Incident had a really specific group of needs that they wanted taken care of, and I was the most passionate about it, so I took on the job as manager/tour promoter," explains Mike. "It was a huge learning process and over the last three years we figured out that we can do it better for them than anyone else because we care the most. The band continues to grow—in three years they've gone from playing for free ski passes on the mountains of Colorado to selling out three nights at the Fillmore in advance, selling to 3,000 to 4,000 people around the country. They've got a diehard group of lunatics that follow them all around and outside of the country.

"The most satisfying thing for me is to know that we actually play a role at the shows. You look at the audience and you see how the music is actually impacting people and how much joy it actually brings to the world. Knowing that you played a small part in making that happen is really rewarding. For us it's about bringing art into the world. It's rare to find people who are truly based on integrity and doing what they believe in . . . and are willing to fight to the mat for what they believe in."

## Branching out Beyond Promotion

If you're booking a tour for a band, you may find yourself getting involved in more aspects of band management out of necessity. There are things that a young band needs done, and they have no one to do them, so they're looking for a hand.

"Slowly we took over every aspect of marketing and promotion for the String Cheese Incident," notes Mike Luba. "We do all of their merchandising because we figure we can do it better. We can keep the money in house and it's worked great. We got chased by all the major record labels, and we decided to start our own label, which has been really successful."

If you take on this responsibility, you're fully responsible for the band's livelihood, but the rewards can be tremendous. Madison House started a travel division simply to make it easier for their fans to get to the shows, because so many people go to multiple shows.

"If they want to fly to see a show somewhere, they can call our office, they can buy the tickets straight from us, they can book their airlines, their hotels, their campgrounds, whatever they want," offers Mike. "The T-shirts, the CDs, anything they want. And it's a real personal family connection with a huge group of people. It's pretty amazing."

## Merchandising

Don't know whether you've noticed it or not, but concert promotion and merchandising seem to go hand in hand. You're already at the gig; you might as well sell T-shirts. It's easy enough to do. Get a staff of established kids who do the art and create the manufacturing. Then offer it through your mail-order catalog, Web site, and a toll-free number.

"A lot of bands make their profits on tour by selling merchandise," offers Vince Reese. "An independent band is mostly selling out of the trunk. They have their own CDs, their own T-shirts. A band could make a tour profitable by selling merchandise and CDs, possibly getting a sponsor—a guitar company or somebody."

If it's an older crowd, usually about 25–30 percent of an audience will buy something. If it's a young, hip band, like the Backstreet Boys, almost half the audience buys something. If there are 30,000 people there, you'll probably sell 15,000 shirts. It's not that half the people are buying shirts, but half the people who are buying are buying two or three T-shirts and a program.

A good merchandising item usually has the artists' picture or logo prominently displayed in front, and it's a shirt that can't be bought in the stores. You want to have the tour name and the year because that's really important to people.

When selling merchandise at shows, be advised that the venue takes different percentages every night—up to about 35 percent of your gross profits at big venues.

"We try not to give the venue anything," notes Mike Luba. "Sometimes it works, sometimes it doesn't. The reality is that I don't ask them for a cut of the bar sales so they shouldn't be asking me for a cut of my merchandising. But they do give us the space to sell our stuff, so between 10 and 20 percent is as much as we'll give up, except when there's an established precedent—like the Fillmore takes 35 percent. It's just been like that for so long that it's non-negotiable. It's not even worth fighting over."

As the band grows, so will the merchandising. When the String Cheese Incident first started out, Madison House Productions would order sixty shirts and they'd last a month. Now they go through thousands of shirts each month.

"The concept is that everything is truly symbiotic and they all feed off of each other and lead to a fully successful whole," notes Mike Luba. "Most bands, they farm out their records to a record company, they farm out their merchandising to a monster like Winterland or Sony Signatures, and there's no accountability for it. For us, if something gets screwed up, we can go directly to the source and fix it immediately. We have total control over quality and the production of it, and it's just so effective. And it cuts out all of the middlemen, which means it's more money for the guys in the band."

# ENTERTAINMENT LAW:
## *I Fought the Law and the Law Won* 𝄇

Certainly doing Janet Jackson's and R.E.M.'s deals were proud moments, just because when you're in that position, you can rewrite the rules of how the game gets played and set new standards for everybody.

—DONALD PASSMAN, ATTORNEY
GANG, TYRE, RAMER & BROWN

*H*ow many stories have you heard about musicians, managers, or agents signing bad deals? More than you can count on your fingers and your toes. Take the twisted tale of the Artist Formerly Known as Prince. Between 1978 and 1996, Prince recorded seventeen albums for Warner Bros., including megahits such as "Purple Rain" and "1999." He got into some bad contracts and lost the rights to everything—including his name. That is why the Artist Formerly Known as Prince is rerecording his entire back catalog for future release online.

Lawyers are a necessity in the music business because all business is based on contractual agreements. A good music industry attorney is knowledgeable about contract law and copyright law in general, and the music industry specifically.

"It's like any other skill," notes entertainment industry attorney Donald Passman, who works with Gang, Tyre, Ramer & Brown and negotiated a $70 million deal for Janet Jackson, and an $80 million contract for R.E.M. "If you aren't doing it day to day, you don't bring the same level of expertise to it, and you don't bring the same sort of relationships and ability to get things done."

Good attorneys should easily be able to identify the rights an artist needs to obtain for any given project. They will then help the band negotiate and draft an agreement protecting their rights. Attorneys can offer insight into what terms a band can expect—how much money the group is likely to generate and how soon they might expect to see any of it. A good attorney is the band's pillar of strength when it comes to dealing with the suits.

> **Commit it to memory:** *Securing the services of an attorney does not guarantee a band the best contract, but it greatly increases their understanding of the business arrangements into which they are entering.*

Attorneys are responsible for a wide range of legal issues, from setting up a band's business structure to reviewing their contracts and protecting their intellectual property. If the band lives long and prospers, their lawyers can achieve a high level of gratification from their work.

"I love working with people," notes Donald Passman. "I like making things happen. I like the marriage of art and commerce. I like taking creative people and helping them relate to business, and taking business people and helping them relate to the creative side. I like being in the middle and getting things done."

## Specializing in Music

Each state has its own laws. Music law is not recognized as an area of specialization by the state board of legal specialization in many states. Consequently, attorneys practicing entertainment law must reveal to a client if they are not board certified in music law.

"When I was in college, I just wanted to be an attorney. I didn't know there was such a thing as a music attorney," offers Donald Passman. "I didn't find out that it existed until I was already in my first year of law school. But I loved music, and I was always around music. I played in bands. My stepfather was a disc jockey. I always knew I had a passion for music. I didn't know I could put the two together until I went to law school."

Attorneys, though licensed to practice law, do not take a designated test or course of study to allow them to be considered specialists in music law—probably because most states do not offer a test for this type of specialty. Most attorneys in entertainment law have gained expertise through self-styled education and practical experience.

"I'd been practicing law for twenty years, and most of my practice involved litigation with criminals," notes Rod Underhill, Esq., legal affairs counselor for MP3.com. "I was interested in representing musicians who couldn't get a break. That's how I got into music law."

You can specialize in entertainment copyright/contract law—which is a great way to break into the music biz. Once upon a time, a good music industry attorney had experience only in the music business. These days, a music industry legal counselor needs experience in handling multimedia licensing and development issues, as well as a traditional background in recording and publishing deal negotiations.

"There is not a lot you can take in law school," Donald stresses, "although almost all of the law schools nowadays have some sort of entertainment law or copyright law class. I took copyright, and I took contracts. Those were probably the two most valuable classes in law school for me. It's a matter of persistence, doing the best you can in law school. Then you have to go out and get a job at a firm where you can get trained. You have to get into the industry, and that's where you can learn the specifics about entertainment law."

## Legal at Labels

If you want to work with a label, as opposed to being an independent counselor, then contract or rights law is definitely a strong way to go. Each record label has about a half-dozen attorneys. A label attorney usually takes on a band for the duration of the time that the attorney is at the label. To advance, label lawyers often have to move back and forth between labels, unless they have a band that breaks—giving them carte blanche with that label. There are relatively few label attorneys. Most entertainment industry attorneys prefer to work with a firm, because that's where the real money is.

"I came to a firm where I could get trained because they were already doing a lot of entertainment work," Donald points out. "The other thing I did was I just went out and met everybody."

## Developing Your Clientele

The best way for an entertainment attorney to develop a reputation is by word of mouth—networking.

"Meet people. That's my advice to anybody getting a start in the business, whatever you want to do," observes Donald. "A lot of the people I met when I got started—who were kids like I was—are now running the companies and are in important positions in the industry."

Being an effective attorney, like everything else in the music business, is all about relationships. Who do you know? Who referred you? It doesn't matter if you're on the label side, or the band side; you need to know people and have them respect you to build a bigger and better clientele.

Developing your clientele comes through advertising and referral. While she's out there establishing herself among her peers, an aggressive music attorney will also be doing a lot of networking, going to clubs, checking out talent, searching for bands—acting very much like a talent scout.

"Bands find me a lot of different ways," reveals entertainment industry attorney Michael Leventhal, a technology/new media partner at Wolf, Rifkin & Shapiro, LLP in Santa Monica, California. "Some bands find me by word of mouth or over the Internet." If a lawyer has a solid network of people in the industry, oftentimes a label or a publisher or a manager or the first person to discover a band will put the lawyer and the band in touch with each other.

"I pick my clients on a bunch of different criteria. I don't take a lot of young bands, although I like to take a few because it's exciting to watch a young band happen," states Donald. "I have to like them and feel like they've got a passion for what they do. It will be based on either a manager or a record company I know who says this person has really got some talent. Or sometimes they come in with five or six companies chasing them, and I get a sense that there is something there."

## An Easy Way to Meet the Right People

If you are considering a career as a lawyer, or if you already have legal training and are looking to switch your career focus, volunteering is always a great way to go. Give time to the arts program in your city. Some lawyer referral services specialize in arts- or entertainment-related law. Among the more prominent of these organizations is California Lawyers for the Arts in San Francisco, Santa Monica, and Oakland. In addition, there are similar Volunteer Lawyers for the Arts offices in Chicago, Atlanta, and New York.

"A substantial portion of my practice was devoted to pro bono work in the entertainment industry," confirms Rod Underhill, Esq. "During that time I represented publishers and artists and writers and musicians, dealing primarily with copyright issues. About two years ago I started concentrating more on representing unsigned artists and developing opportunities more on unsigned artists. The odds were they couldn't afford to pay for the services of an attorney and, without my help, they wouldn't get very far."

Typically, these nonprofit services charge a nominal administrative fee to refer the client to an attorney for a free or low-cost initial consultation. Many of these organizations also provide regular workshops and

clinics, which are informative and provide yet another method of networking with attorneys.

# Working with Young Bands

Young musicians don't need a lot of people on their team, but they definitely *do* need people who can talk and think money—people like lawyers
and accountants. A good business guy or two working on a band's behalf
is the starting point for a great team.

An attorney's role with an evolving band is critical. In addition to
providing negotiation skills and general legal counsel, attorneys often
serve as business advisors and professional matchmakers, bringing parties
together for new projects. Additionally, attorneys administer copyrights
and collect and receive funds on behalf of their clients. And, of course,
when deals go sour, an attorney coordinates the litigation process to
resolve the claim.

In many cases, you're like a good friend to the band, looking out for
their best interests and helping them along in their career by just knowing the people you know. And you'll feel the rewards of being a good
friend when the connections pay off and you have a platinum band under
your wing.

If a band can meet your fees, that's great, but be sure the group is
easy to deal with. If the band grows into anything noteworthy, you'll probably end up working with them on a semi-regular basis, so you should
make sure that the band members are not particularly difficult personalities, as exemplified by lawsuit-heavy bands like Guns N' Roses, Nirvana,
and Stone Temple Pilots. Hopefully, the band members are people you can
relate to on a personal level.

As a member of the band's team, you, the lawyer, should like the
music and find it commercially viable. It should also be something you can
easily shop to your contacts.

The primary service that most young bands require from an attorney is shopping a deal with a record label. For this you've got to know people in the business, since record labels typically do not accept unsolicited
material. All A&R submissions come from somebody they know—from
lawyers or managers who are acquaintances of the label executives.

There are three ways to be compensated for shopping a band:

1. An up-front flat fee
2. A percentage of the deal
3. A contingent flat fee, payable upon closure of the deal

The most popular form of attorney compensation for getting a band a record deal is method number two: taking a percentage of the deal. If the agreement is to take 10 percent of the artist's income, it should be made clear to which sources of income the percentage is applied. Is it applied to a percentage of the advance, the first record, or the entire deal? Are these ancillary income sources like merchandising and tour revenues?

## What to Charge the Band

Like everything else in the music business, fee structures can vary wildly, depending on your network of contacts, your location, and your experience. There are several ways to be compensated by the bands you represent:

1. Bill on a simple hourly rate. Generally, attorneys charge between $150 and $350 an hour. Flat-fee billing is used by some attorneys for specific projects, such as incorporating, registering a trademark, or registering songs with rights agencies.
2. Charge a percentage—something like 5 percent of the gross. "Lawyers might work on hourly, they might work on percentage," observes Michael Leventhal. "It's more likely to be a percentage on everything the artist makes, less certain types of deductions. What types of deductions? For example, if the artist is going to get $250,000 to record the album, and all of that is actually going to go into production. The lawyer and the manager probably won't take part of that money because the artist is never actually going to see that money."
3. Do value billing, which is becoming more common in the music industry. Value billing means that at the conclusion of the deal, the attorney asks for a fee that is based on the extent of the services rendered and the size and nature of the deal. If you're going to practice value billing, you have to establish some up-front parameters for this kind of arrangement.

When a band signs the legal services agreement, it's standard that they pay an up-front retainer deposit, which is typically held in trust and applied against fees and expenses as they accrue. Expenses, by the way, are usually billable and may include messengers, fax, regular and overnight mail, long-distance phone calls, and photocopies.

## Know Your Rights

Once a band is signed, and those months of preliminary contract work—we're talking hundreds of pages of contracts here—are out of the way, one of a lawyer's main responsibilities to a band is to protect their rights.

In today's media-intensive world, there are a lot of different rights to protect and a lot of advice to be given. Most artists don't really understand what the issues are. Legal representation is not about getting you the most money—it's about guaranteeing your career. The average life span of an artist's career is about as long as that of an NFL quarterback. That is, their careers don't last very long. If a band makes a deal that screws them and puts them on the shelf for seven years—which is how long a typical record contract has an artist bound to a label—by the time the talents get out of that contract and are able to make music again, their window of opportunity may have passed and their potential market may have already graduated into the working world.

George Michael is a good example of an artist who got caught up in a bad contract while his career was flying high. He had a six-year battle with his record label, Columbia. Once the label was bought by the Japanese conglomerate Sony in 1989, George felt he was not getting adequate representation and promotion. It took him $14 million to get out of his deal. He survived to release *Older* on DreamWorks in 1997. George Michael was one of the very lucky ones. Only the really exceptional artists manage to survive the various trends and establish themselves as serious artists over a long period.

A band lawyer should do his best to keep the band from getting into a situation where they miss their opportunity because they're in dispute with their record label for three years.

## Ways to Handle Disputes

Few business problems are so terrible that they must involve lawsuits. If you're working on behalf of a band, and an altercation arises, why lose years and years off the band's life by going to court when there are other ways of reaching an agreement? As the band's lawyer, it is your job to give them the best possible advice so they don't get caught up in the court system. Generally speaking, legal problems evolve out of misunderstandings. Sometimes talking the problem out with an impartial mediator can resolve a messy situation before it gets seriously out of hand.

### *Mediation*

As an alternative to hiring a lawyer to go to court, mediation is a great, low-key, nonconfrontational way to settle most arguments. Mediation does not result in an ultimatum or impose an outcome on the disputing parties. Instead, the mediator attempts to negotiate a solution that satisfies all parties involved.

The mediator may attempt to:

- Help negotiators realistically assess alternatives
- Encourage flexibility
- Shift the focus from the past to the future
- Prompt the parties to come up with creative settlements
- Invent solutions that meet the fundamental interests of all parties

Traditionally, the mediator meets in separate confidential sessions with the conflicting parties. During these sessions, the mediator comes to understand the different positions of the disputees. Solutions are discussed, and then the mediator takes an agreed-upon position to the other party, after first listening to the other party's position.

Other than being an unbiased set of ears, mediators tend to enter disputes with minimal authority. Their ability to bring about constructive movement or settlement depends on the willingness of the parties to accept the mediator. Oftentimes, a respected mediator who has no expertise in the area of dispute may be more successful than an issue-savvy mediator who does not have the parties' respect.

Mediation is a less formal, less time-consuming, and less expensive way to go, and lawyers need not be involved. Mediation is more about talking through the dispute and finding a creative solution to keep future relations easy and satisfying for both parties. Mediation is a good way to resolve conflicts in the entertainment industry, with its unusual structure and requests, and it is flexible enough to accommodate any industry or practice, assuming the parties themselves have chosen a mediator who is up to the task.

As an attorney, you might want to think about including a mediation clause in a contract or agreement. This allows for conflicts to be resolved early in the process, before parties become adversarial.

Most bands are generally afraid of lawyers, and when given a choice between mediation and arbitration, they'll choose the less formal course of mediation.

### Arbitration

Another method of settling a problematic situation is arbitration. In an arbitration, the intermediary carries a lot more weight. Arbitration means referring a dispute to a neutral third party, usually a lawyer, who is empowered to make a decision based on the issues presented to him. Unlike mediation, which takes a casual approach, arbitration contains the essential elements of a court appearance: Proofs and arguments are submitted to a neutral individual who has the power to issue a decision that is binding on the parties. The arbitrator essentially acts like a judge but, unlike a judge, holds only the authority granted to her by the arbitration clause in the contract.

The key issues in arbitration are:

- How many arbitrators will decide on the issue
- Who the arbitrator is
- Which issues will be resolved
- Whether the decision will come with a reasoned legal opinion or only a short award statement
- What rules apply, whether there will be remuneration, and how much
- Whether the arbitrator's decision will bind the parties

Guidelines for these issues should be established before a dispute arises. Additionally, rules should be laid out in boilerplate contractual language agreed to by the parties and/or in union or guild contracts. Such contract language frequently can be found through organizations such as the American Arbitration Association, J.A.M.S./Endispute, Inc., and Arts Arbitration and Mediation Services (part of the California Lawyers for the Arts organization).

An arbitration may not ease the tension between those in dispute because there is a combative element to the resolution—a winner and loser, so to speak. The entertainment field requires genuine participation to accomplish a project, and arbitration does not necessarily promote reconciliation and participation.

## Preparing for Negotiations

Attorney Sloane Smith Morgan, Esq., advises that the band or lawyer have "a written negotiation worksheet prior to starting any negotiation session." There are several issues to be aware of when entering into any entertainment-related negotiation, including:

- Who are the parties and what does each party want?
- What are the priorities?
- What are the opponent's goals?
- Is competitive or cooperative negotiation the way to go?
- What strategy will you use: a bidding strategy or a win-win solution?

Knowing the course you're going to take in your negotiations is critical to a successful outcome.

# Job Satisfaction

"I've gotten more interested in working with bands after their careers started to peter out," says Rod Underhill. "Some of my clients have been formerly platinum-selling artists that I've helped at the tail end of their career. A lot of what I've done is to help find session work and actually earn a living. I do this primarily for musicians who are not songwriters and do not have publishing catalogs behind them to bring them continued income. Helping them makes me feel like I'm doing something worthwhile."

Most attorneys who do pro bono work to help artists have a conscience and take satisfaction in helping those in need. As we all know, the benefits of being an attorney can be mighty. Attorneys make great money—that's the reason a lot of people go into law. If you want the guarantee of a hefty salary, if you like paying attention to details, and you have a confrontational nature, this is a really good line of work for you.

# *Music Publishing* 𝄆

If you don't support the artist and the musician, and they can't
afford their art, the foundation will erode and you will have an
erosion of the intellectual establishment.

—VINCE CASTELLUCCI, SENIOR DIRECTOR OF LICENSING

THE HARRY FOX AGENCY

*I*f you can't be the artist, help the artist. If you can't be in the limelight, there's nothing more exciting than to be around the limelight. Being involved with a musician's moneymaking process
will help get you into the limelight—not to mention that the
musician needs you desperately. Such are the joys and satisfactions of
music publishing.

What exactly does a music publisher do? Perhaps the simplest definition is that a music publisher seeks to maximize the circulation, the
impact, and the financial profitability of songs and to coach and mentor
promising writers.

Music publishing is the term used to describe the exploitation of the
myriad of royalties and income sources that derive from the copyright to
a song. The music publishing company is the entity responsible for issu-
ing licenses and collecting royalties for the songwriter. Publishing has
been the major source of revenue for songwriters since the turn of the
century and is an important component of every artist's business that
should not be ignored. One hit song can result in millions of dollars in
publishing income.

There are four general categories of revenue derived by music publishing: performance income, mechanical rights income, sheet music income, and synchronization income.

It would be incredibly burdensome for a music publisher to license directly to every radio station, concert hall, TV station, club, and restaurant that wishes to play songs that the publisher owns. To accommodate the publishers and songwriters and alleviate the impracticality of licensing, several companies—known as performing rights organizations—have come forward to handle licensing and royalty collection on a massive scale. These companies include the American Society of Composers, Authors, and Publishers (ASCAP) and Broadcast Music Incorporated (BMI).

In everyday practice, the radio stations, television stations, and other public performance outlets pay a royalty to the performing rights organizations. Then, after deducting an administrative fee, these organizations distribute performance royalty revenue to their members based on the number of times their works have been performed. In other words, these organizations handle the difficult task of collecting public performance income nationwide and then distributing it in proportion to the success of each composition.

Music publishing is also a complex subject. At its foundation are the laws of copyright. At the periphery are copublishing agreements, performing rights organizations, and compulsory mechanical licenses. It is a large and intricate industry involving thousands of songs and billions of dollars. It's a satisfying business because if musicians received no royalties they would get sick of surviving on tuna fish and ketchup soup and find other jobs and, consequently, the quality of music in the marketplace would plummet.

"By staying in corporate, I'm trying my darnedest to keep my habit of listening to great music going by making sure that the music is properly licensed by the record companies and that the rights to the songs are not owned by the conglomerates," declares Vince Castellucci, former studio and touring musician, now the senior director of licensing at the Harry Fox Agency in New York. "I make sure that those royalties are paid and they're fulfilled."

> **Did you know:** *The song that is sold the most times is the Irving Berlin song "White Christmas." There isn't another song that even approaches that one when it comes to recorded popular sales.*

# How Do You Get into Publishing?

Although music publishing and licensing is satisfying, it's not a line of work that people usually dream of getting into. It's a line of work they fall into through odd or circuitous circumstances.

"An editor suggested I talk to the head of the West Coast office at BMI since they were looking for a publicist," recalls Hanna Bolte, now the senior director of media relations for BMI. "When I went in and talked to them, I was not really serious about the job. I was working at a record company at the time and didn't really want to leave that end of the business. But, economics within the industry were shaky and I thought this would be the most prudent thing for me to do—go to work for a company that was stable and offered more job security than a label could. It's turned out to be a great career choice."

Vince Castellucci was managing an R&B group, the Persuasions, until the baritone, Rhodes, died of a brain embolism. Vince decided to chill out and to reorganize, and at the same time Harry Fox made him an offer to work in the synchronization department in his firm—get it up and running and make it profitable.

"It tumble-weeded after that," Vince proclaims. "The company kept growing in publisher representation and we were constantly trying to do a good job for our publishers."

# How Does Publishing Make Money?

Publishing is certainly not boring—you're dealing with lots of artists, lots of music, and lots of diverse details. You won't go into publishing knowing everything about it—you will learn by asking questions. And you will have to learn a good deal of financial information because there is a lot of money in music publishing. It's one of the most lucrative sides of the music industry.

A variety of rights come along with a record deal. Some need to be transferred, some need to be retained. The first two rights that need to be addressed are the *underlying composition* rights for any song that the artist may write, and the rights to the *sound recording* itself.

> ***Commit it to memory:*** *One recorded song has two sets of copyrights, both of which must be protected.*

When you hear a song on the radio, TV, cable, and so on, the songwriter is receiving a *broadcast royalty*. When you purchase a CD, the artist receives a *mechanical royalty*. Broadcast royalties are paid to a tune's songwriters, composers, and music publishers. This is split into two shares—the writer's share and the publisher's share.

"BMI pays from a 200 percent system. One hundred percent goes to the songwriter and 100 percent goes to the publisher," says Hanna Bolte. "If there is no publisher assigned, then that 100 percent rolls over to the songwriter's share. Regardless of who is assigned what percentage, it has to equal 200 percent."

However, when a band enters into a record deal, they're really talking about the rights to the sound recording, not the right to the underlying composition. In a standard major label recording deal, the label pays for recording and owns the copyright to the sound recording. The underlying composition rights—the actual rights to the song—are owned by the artist in conjunction with the publishing company.

Mechanical income is paid to the publisher by the company that is manufacturing the recordings under a contract clause called a "mechanical license." The closest organization to a mechanical rights society is the Harry Fox Agency. Like ASCAP, BMI, and SESAC, Harry Fox collects mechanical royalties for compositions that are in his catalog, deducting a small administrative fee, and remitting the remainder to the music publisher.

For example, every time an album with the song "I Heard It Through the Grapevine" is sold, the writers—Norman Whitfield and Barrett Strong—divide 7.1 cents.

The Harry Fox Agency has more than thirty different licenses, including synchronization multimedia and karaoke licenses. The synchronization rates are negotiable . . . which is how the Rolling Stones got Microsoft to pay $12 million for the rights to use the song "Start Me Up" to promote Windows 95. Harry Fox currently represents 20,000 music publishers.

"I fix a lot of things," explains Vince Castellucci. "My primary duty is to license and secondarily I collect royalties and distribute them to the publishers Harry Fox represents."

BMI, one of the largest music publishers in the country, was founded in 1940 as a nonprofit corporation representing songwriters and composers of all genres who were not being represented on radio. Many of them were not eligible under the membership guidelines of the older American performing rights societies. BMI offered first-time representation to songwriters of blues, jazz, R&B, gospel, folk, country, Spanish-language, and other types of American music.

BMI currently represents over 200,000 songwriters, composers, and music publishers. The company is now one of three performing rights organizations in the United States. The other two organizations are ASCAP and SESAC. Performing rights organizations (PROs) collect and distribute broadcast royalties to their songwriters, composers, and music publishers. They also collect licensing fees for the "public performances" of their repertoires—including radio airplay, broadcast and cable television airings, and live and recorded performances by all other music customers, including but not limited to the Internet, restaurants, retail outlets, music-on-hold, and the like.

A music publishing company can represent one artist, as in the case of Lanni Tunes, Finger Eleven's publishing company, or it can be a record-label worth of material, such as PolyGram International Publishing. Publishing companies can be highly desirable, and are often bought and sold (which is why Michael Jackson owned the rights to many Beatles' songs). They're referred to as highly acquisitionable.

Publishing catalogs are money builders, slow and steady, but constant and consistent. BMG Music Publishing, which was founded in 1987, controls copyrights to more than 700,000 songs worldwide. Since its formation, the company has made some 150 music publishing acquisitions, including the catalogs of such diverse and internationally respected songwriters and artists as the Beach Boys, B. B. King, Barry Manilow, John Hiatt, Santana, Boz Scaggs, Vinicius de Moraes, and Toquinho. In addition, the company has purchased major catalogs, including Belgium's World Music, the U.K.'s E.G. Music, Italy's Blue Flower, and Germany's Jack White.

"It's very interesting to study copyright law because there are so many nuances; it's not cut and dry," admits Vince. "U.S. copyright law is just that—it's for the U.S. Then you have German copyright law, Italian copyright law. It's statutory; it's for that country."

From a music publishing perspective, each one of a copyright's exclusive rights can be transformed into a publishing income source.

## Copyright Law

Copyrights are at the heart of music publishing. They infuse and drive all of music publishing's different sources of income and revenue. The source of all U.S. copyright law is the U.S. Constitution: "The Congress shall have power . . . to promote the Progress of Science and useful Arts, by securing for limited Times to Authors and Inventors the exclusive right to their respective Writings and Discoveries" (U.S. Constitution, Article I, Section 8, Clause 8).

In less archaic terms, the Constitution grants to authors a limited-duration monopoly in their works. This monopoly and its particular forms and rights are controlled by the U.S. Congress and can be found in codified form at 17 U.S.C. §1 et seq. The time of ownership on a catalog used to be seventy-five years, but the expiration of copyrights on early Mickey Mouse films helped push Congress to extend the period of copyright ownership to ninety-five years.

The purpose of copyright law is to create an economic incentive for authors to create new works by granting a monopoly in those works to the author for a limited time. The important component of this economic incentive is the monopoly itself. The presence of a monopoly prevents third parties from taking or using the author's intellectual property without obtaining permission and, more important for the author, paying a royalty.

The copyright owner has the exclusive right to do or to authorize a third party to: (1) reproduce the copyrighted work; (2) prepare derivative works based on the copyrighted work; (3) distribute copies of the copyrighted work to the public; (4) perform publicly certain forms of copyrighted works; and (5) publicly display certain forms of copyrighted works. (See 17 U.S.C. §106.)

## A Day in the Life of a Performing Rights Professional

A typical day in the life of someone in the performing rights business is varied. Often, it entails talking to songwriters who're trying to get more exposure, or to an unsigned band who would like to get on an industry showcase. You could deal with television and film composers regarding how to promote their work. It could be administrative duties—making sure that songwriters and composers have submitted the correct forms or at least understand how to fill them out. It's taking calls from the general public regarding what the company does and does not do.

The strengths of performing rights organizations include helping a band find an agent, a manager, a lawyer, or a music publishing house, but their real forte is more along the lines of artist empowerment—helping musicians make the most of their careers.

"We offer a lot of various educational outreach services to try to help our songwriters learn the business, as well as promotional events to help showcase their talent," offers Hanna. "Because we work with so many different industries, we can help songwriters matriculate through the industry—be an ally for them."

Working on the financial side of the music business may not lead to name recognition, but the jobs are certainly vital to the industry, and you may actually brush elbows with more "glamour" than you would working on the artistic side of the business. While the corporate side of the music business involves attending ritzy charity functions honoring executives in the industry, the music side has a higher grunge factor, where you might be more likely to take the artist out to the Rainbow for pizza or hit the road to promote a band's appearance in cities across the country.

"The corporate side of this business is just that—the business of music," confirms Hanna. "While music is the driving force behind all of us—and our passion for it got all of us to where we are today—working on this side of the fence is about business—understanding how songwriters make money."

## Why Publishing Is Unique

When you're working with rights instead of bands, the whole way you look at the music business changes.

"It's more of a corporate imaging—but it has a lot of outreach," explains Hanna Bolte. "I can work on advertising, on marketing, help our government relations VP out with a campaign to target Congressmen via states or the federal government. I can work directly with our composers. I can work with a baby band who wants to sign up with BMI. I can work with our showcase series, I can work with our licensing department—especially when it comes to the Internet. I can work with our Latin division. There are so many areas I deal with on a day-to-day basis. BMI has many products that we are promoting: We're always trying to make people understand and come aboard and be a BMI songwriter, composer, or music publisher."

## Publishing Companies

The mechanics of a publishing company are fairly simple. A songwriter assigns her copyright to the song (or her portion of the copyright in the song) to the publisher. In return, the publisher agrees to be responsible for the business facets of music publishing—in other words, to administer the publishing. Additionally, the publisher agrees to pay the songwriter based on the royalties it collects, typically on a 50-50 split excluding performance and sheet income.

The mechanics of music publishing remain constant regardless of the publisher's size. The main task of the publisher is purely administrative: The company obtains and registers the copyrights to its songs, it clears the songs with its performing rights organization, it issues licenses, collects royalties, and pays the songwriters according to their publishing agreements. A number of publishers also actively shop their songs to artists looking to get them recorded or to moviemakers seeking to place them in a major motion picture. Additionally, some publishers will also actively work with their songwriters to improve their songwriting ability.

## Specialized Publishing Companies

Whereas publishing companies like Warner/Chappell will publish virtually any song, other publishers are more specialized. The Hildegard Publishing

Company was founded in 1988 to promote and preserve the music of women composers of the past and present, shaping a music heritage for generations to come.

Hildegard Publishing started with 6 items listed in its first catalog, which has grown to more than 450 entries—including music for piano, harpsichord, harp, and organ; vocal and choral music; string, woodwind, and brass chamber music; orchestral music; CDs; and music for young people.

Another example of specialized publishing is the BriLee Music Publishing Company, which specializes in junior high, middle school, and elementary choral music.

## The Most Satisfying Aspects of Publishing

A career in publishing is unpredictable and varied, and yields a strong sense of accomplishment.

"Diversity is one of my key words here," notes Hanna. "There are so many different areas that I work with—Internet, licensing, government relations, individual songwriters and composers, film music, community events, charity events, awards dinners, writing columns for magazines, conventions, showcases—the list goes on and on. We support a variety of causes because we represent a wide variety of songwriters."

Publishing allows you to be a conduit for information for a lot of writers and composers. In a way, it's like teaching the artists how to have a career in music. You share with them information about the business end of the company that they may not know.

"We're usually the first point before they get a record deal and before they go on to greatness," confides Hanna. "It's a good educational point for them. They start to get an idea, a road map of what to expect."

Vince Castellucci appreciates the fact that working in publishing lets him see the music industry grow. "Seeing that it's healthy, alive, and vibrant, seeing that deals are constantly being made with artists and financial institutions," he enthuses. "Seeing that publishing companies are helping, because they are being bought up by the majors, seeing that the smaller companies are healthy."

## How the Web Is Changing Publishing

Recognizing that the future of the music business will include online distribution and sales, performing rights organizations are designing a series of technological initiatives that will form the core of the music copyright industry's digital development agenda for the next two years.

On tap for implementation in the near future are a number of technical advances, including online works registration for songwriters, composers, and music publishers; secure exclusive Web domains for songwriters, allowing them to review their catalogs, update account information, and make inquiries; secure download of royalty information for publishers; and a dedicated full-time client service team.

These global copyright information systems initiatives include the development of a next-generation architecture for a global "virtual database" of musical works, permitting performing rights societies to exchange information directly among their mainframe computers. Companies like BMI and ASCAP have taken a leadership role in the development of the prototype for this virtual database, and remain dedicated to the development of the common information system.

Suddenly, exposing a band's music to a new client is simple. In the new world of e-commerce, the process is short and sweet. If an advertiser is looking for a song for Web commercials, he goes to publishing houses on the Internet, looks at the song titles, selects the songs, even listens to sound samples. If the advertiser likes the song, he goes to the publisher and makes a deal. This is all done by e-mail, Internet, and phone. Awesome. The copyright owner of the song recording can instantaneously download sixty seconds or the whole thing from a digitally perfect online copy. The advertiser's editors go right into the production room, punch it in, edit it right there, and they're done within an hour instead of waiting weeks or months to get clearance, get the master recording, and reedit it.

But, of course, the Web is simplifying the whole process of selling and reselling music. Absolutely.

# MEDIA AND PUBLICITY:
## *Let Me Tell You*

I want to make a difference in helping change the way music is going one more time. Going from Guns N' Roses to Nirvana was such an incredible high, we were changing popular culture. I would love to have another ride like I've had with Queen or Guns N' Roses or Nirvana. It's the best drug known to man.

—BRYN BRIDENTHAL, HEAD OF PUBLICITY
DREAMWORKS RECORDS

## Spreading the Word

The publicist is the liaison between the artist and the media. Media includes newspapers, magazines, radio, the Web, and TV that specialize in music and entertainment, and/or feature interviews with different artists and bands. The publicist acts as the contact between the artist and those media. The publicist will pitch a story or interview about an artist to the media, and if someone in the media responds positively, a time will be set so that the journalist or editor can learn the artist's story. Hopefully, a bond is formed and positive promotion for the artist goes flying into everybody's home.

"As publicists, what we're really all about is figuring out a way to bring music to the masses," emphasizes Mitch Schneider, founder of MSO Public Relations, a publicity agency that likes to work with edgy people, from Alanis Morissette to David Bowie, Korn, Green Day, and Dwight Yoakum. "The way to do that is through the media, and media would encompass everything from newspapers to magazines to radio syndication to television outlets and the whole Internet world. We reach out to all the press in those areas and hopefully inspire them to create pieces on our artists."

The publicist determines the musical genre the artist or band fits into—whether it's hard rock, New Age, punk, ska, surf, mainstream, or whatever—and then contacts the appropriate outlets. Each genre has its own specialists—writers and photographers who love a certain kind of music, or who are just music enthusiasts in general. Get these folks excited about your client, and they could break the artist to the world with just one feature article, cover photo, or centerfold interview.

## Media

It's the publicist's job to know what audience each media outlet caters to, and to get publicity for his artists in the appropriate marketplace. A good publicist will inspire the media in more than one area—newspapers, magazines, radio syndication, TV—to spawn coverage, including feature stories, reviews, factoids, and tidbits.

"I call myself a media arsonist. On a good day we throw some really good matches out there and they catch," declares Mitch Schneider.

"The most important thing to do when you sign clients is to sit down with them," advises Mitch. "It sounds so basic it's ridiculous, but that's really how you do it. You figure out what is true to them, what really turns them on, how they want to be perceived in the media. It's very important to just let the artists talk and really just explain to you their vision."

"It's all about image," confirms Jim Heath, founder of the Reverend Horton Heat. "I'm not really in the business of marketing—I just play guitar and sing in a band. 'It's Martini Time' was the theme for the whole *It's Martini Time* CD, and it has grown to be the theme for the band. There are a lot of marketing gimmicks that the record company comes up with around that. I'm like, 'Oh, y'all want to do that? Fine. Y'all want to spend money on that? Great!' How I present myself is not something that I came up with."

> **Commit it to memory:** *The people who are going to work hardest to get the word out about a band are the publicists, and the ones who are going to help the group spread the word the fastest are the media.*

## Publicity

Media and publicity are rather glamorous and exciting areas because your job is to put the artist in the spotlight. You do lunch, you travel to TV tapings, you supervise media events.

"What I love about the job is the process, the actual packaging of information—in essence, being a news bureau," offers Bryn Bridenthal of DreamWorks. "I love dealing with artists, and I love trying to get them to trust me, and have some sort of understanding. I love the psychological games.

"It's a very satisfying area of work because you see tangible results (TV appearances, magazine articles) for your work. You can watch the band's career grow. There's nothing in life more fun than going with a band from zero to gold and helping people realize their fantasies. You watch them grow, and watch the lights come on in their eyes as they reach each new plateau."

As a member of the publicity team, there are three ways to measure how much you're going to enjoy working on a project:

1. the music
2. the artist
3. the management

If you like one aspect, you're going to have a good time because you're going to feel like you are providing a service for a good person (or cause). If you like two areas, then you're having more fun than somebody should be paid to have. And if you like all three of them, you're probably going to get heavily involved and have no life whatsoever.

## The Downside to Working Closely with Artists

There are other ways publicity can be all-consuming. All publicists have been out until three in the morning on a semi-regular basis. If you're looking for a normal life, publicity is not for you, because you'll have to make choices. Your friends and family will have to get used to you working all the time. "You don't have to worry much about having a personal life or maintaining anything like that," adds Bryn.

"In the music business, if you try and just put your toe in, it's incredibly frustrating," she admits. "You can't get swept down the stream if you only put your toe in. You have to get wet enough so the current can carry you away."

There are other late-night interruptions—things happening during hours when no one should be doing business. Most veteran publicists have also gotten the 4 A.M. phone call—which inevitably means there's trouble.

"I tell artists, 'Please, call me in the middle of the night if you get arrested, because if it goes on the wires before I can get our story on the wires, that's the story that's going to go,'" notes Bryn. "If you're there first, ahead of the curve, you can make people believe your point of view.

"I got to work with George Michael's episode in the park [his arrest for having sex in a men's room in Central Park]. I had a grand time doing that. I love a good disaster. That's when a publicist really matters."

Bryn recalls getting a call at about ten o'clock in the morning from Michael's manager asking what they could do that day that would go around the world. Most newspapers wouldn't run until the next day. Most television wasn't global enough. It was decided that CNN would be the fastest way with the biggest bang, so Bryn arranged a CNN interview. It had the advantage of going out internationally that night.

George Michael told the story in his own words, using humor and subtlety to defuse the situation. He confessed his sins, apologized, and let everyone get on with their lives.

"Working with George was fabulous because he's so smart, and he used humor well. It was exciting and thrilling and had to be done in a really short period of time."

## What It Takes

"I'm extraordinarily flexible," admits Bryn. "There's no way I could deal with those kinds of acts—from Beck to Hole to Rob Zombie to Guns N' Roses, Aerosmith, and Pat Metheny—and make that many changes in my mindsets if I was rigid."

As a publicist or marketing person, you tend to cover a wide array of music. They say the secret to being able to evolve from one musical genre to another is to have an open mind, and to keep it as fresh as possible.

The publicist must have a clear idea of what an artist or a band is about in order to get that idea across to the media. She'll need to get to know her client and understand the music he makes so that she can guide him in his choices and package the best story about him. Some artists will want to be very involved in the creation of publicity materials out of fear that they will not be presented in the way that they want. It's the publicist's job to get as much information as possible and to keep an open ear to the artists' needs.

"On our first record I was under the impression, 'Well, the label has an art department, they'll pick out photographers, they'll pick out record designers,'" notes Scott Lucas of the platinum-selling band Local H. "It was the kind of thing, 'Well, what do I know about this stuff? Let them do it.' When you do that, it may turn out fine, but, on the other hand, it may not reflect the band's personality.

"We started taking a pretty active roll in the process after the first record. Once we saw a couple of things that weren't up to what we would have liked, it was a pretty big motivator in making us wake up and take control of things."

An exceptional media person lives on the edge—the bow of the ship, the side that's cutting the water. That's where the excitement is. You have to be able to brave the waves. Too often people operate out of fear. To work well with artists, you must be strong and fearless.

If you go in to meet with a brand new group and they sense fear, they will make your life a living hell. You must be unflappable, unstoppable—and you must understand where the band is coming from. An ideal relationship can be forged when the band believes the publicist is protecting them. Once the publicist has earned a band's trust, she can get them to do almost any promotion.

"You'd think that if a record company signed you, they'd want you the way you are, but it turns out that that's not the way it is. They want their own version of what happens to be hot," counters the skeptical Scott Lucas. "If a label tried to make us someone else, we would say, 'Who are you talking about? Just forget about this.' We have to be who we are. We don't want whatever haircut happens to be popular at the time. If you set yourself up to be timeless, in the end that is a better business decision than a label trying to make a band out to be whatever the flavor of the moment is."

## The Effects of Marketing and Promotion

Publicists package information in order to get a reporter's attention. The journalist then interviews the artist and writes about the experience—not just the music, but the personality and the story behind it. If the artist or the band spends the time to figure out what that story is and serves up the information, the journalist is more likely to respond.

"We come up with marketing ideas, even down to bios," offers Scott Lucas. "They get these people who don't really know you to write bios about you and they don't really have much respect for you. It's better not to let people who don't know you take control of things like that. As far as the posters go, you're the one who's going to have to look at it. If you don't like the way you're being represented, then you should do something about it. . . . We'll come up with ideas and we'll get somebody that we like and they'll help us do them."

Getting a band adequate media coverage to help them break is a multipronged effort involving everyone. The process can be time-consuming, and it must be focused. Let's take a make-believe band. We have a group that's hard rock, with a little bit of alternative in there. The publicist sends out advance cassettes three or four months before the album comes out, and that starts the publicity rolling. The publicist approaches the critics at key publications like *Rolling Stone, Spin, Musician, Time, Newsweek*—the gatekeepers of taste. These publications will usually wait and see how the artist does in the marketplace before they give their opinion on it.

The record company may then say, "It seems as if we don't have a critical winner. Let's up the radio promotion."

When you up the radio promotion budget, more airplay potentially should result. When a publicist can go back to the media for round two, and say, "Hi! This is so-and-so following up on that CD we sent you, and it's now getting airplay. It's on thirty to fifty radio stations, a combination of rock and alternative radio around the country, and it's starting to really take."

The journalist asks, "Are they touring?"

The publicist goes back to the label and says, "The press is asking about a tour."

When a band you're promoting goes on the road, a publicist's job gets that much easier. The media is now given the opportunity to see the band, and suddenly a whole new strata of media becomes available. Local newspapers and fanzines won't talk to a band unless they're going to be in that city.

"Touring is very, very important," confirms Scott Stapp, vocalist for the triple-platinum band Creed. "Putting a face behind the songs and developing that intimate relationship with our fans. Our marketing approach was to use a word-of-mouth, grassroots-type of growth. It worked. Local newspapers and fanzines would write, 'You need to go see Creed, they put on a really good show.'"

When it comes to marketing and promoting a band, the record company needs to think about radio promotion, tour support, a video. You're looking at more than $500,000 to break a band, not including advertising and flying the group around for promotion, such as sending a group to New York City for a press junket for three to four nights.

## Independent Publicists

Marketing and publicity are flexible areas with an equal number of people working inside and outside the record company. Ideally, a label would like to keep its publicity in-house to keep expenses down. But if a label is releasing a dozen albums a month in different genres, things can slip through the cracks.

"An outside publicist gets hired for a variety of reasons," explains Mitch Schneider. "Sometimes the artists feel that the record company is being pressured by the full release schedule and they're not necessarily sensitive twenty-four hours a day, so we'll get hired for that. If there's a high-maintenance artist who eats up a sizable amount of the in-house publicist's time, we'll get called as well."

Independent publicists are paid in a variety of different ways. Sometimes they're hired by the band or the artist. Other times they're hired by the record company, which feels overwhelmed because they have a lot of projects going, and they want to put more juice onto something. Sometimes there will be a split: The artist may cover half and the record company may cover half.

"Usually we work with bands who are signed to labels—either a major label, or a reputable indie," notes Mitch. "Our rates vary, based on time consumption. Some bands might only want a punkzine campaign; they don't want to be pitched to *David Letterman* or *Saturday Night Live*. So there are different rates to reflect each band's needs."

## Which Media Are Most Important

Different forms of media serve different purposes. It depends on the artist and it depends on the music—for some, the print media exposure may be critically important; for others it may be incidental. It's incidental if the artist is really a radio act who's all about radio airplay and doesn't have much in the way of personality, or is really mainstream, safe, or conservative. Celine Dion and Neil Diamond are perfect examples of radio-friendly artists who have gotten relatively little media attention.

Press can sell records in some genres of music, such as hard rock, electronic, anything clearly defined and narrowcast. With anything on the fringes, press can really make a difference. The fundamental element that print media offers is a connection with the artist. After you read a well-written article on an act, you feel as if you know them. It's the illusion of intimacy. Like, Wow! They're really speaking to you.

Case in point: A consumer reacts to a single from an artist. It's a great single, but the consumer doesn't buy into the artist because he doesn't feel for him, or have a sense of knowing the act at all. Next time, if the artist puts out a single the consumer doesn't particularly like, the consumer is onto the next thing because no connection was made. If publicity has massaged the media and the consumer has a relationship with the artist, he will in all likelihood forgive the artist for that boring second single, maybe even forgive the artist for two more singles, because the consumer now feels that he "knows" the artist. What publicity has done is create the illusion that there's a relationship between the artist and the consumer. The Web has made that relationship even more intimate and more important.

The most effective medium right now is television because you hear the music, you see the artist, you get a feel for the personality.

"We got the Deftones on *Conan O'Brien,* and that's the type of show that does not ordinarily book really hard bands," proclaims Mitch Schneider. "We fought for that booking for two years. It was the right song—'Be Quiet and Drive.' This great booking helped their sales—their album sold a couple thousand more copies as a result of that TV booking. That makes me proud as a publicist when we can make a mark on something."

TV offers exposure to a broad audience, but the thing that's tough about television is that you don't get repetition, and repetition is really what imprints a song on people's brains. That's what you get from radio—you get repetitions, over and over and over until you can't forget the song.

Print gives the artist an identity. You get to see the personality, you get to read about the personality, but you don't hear the music. It's the Internet that allows a band to be many things to many people.

"When our album *Mr. Funny Face* was released, there was a total media blitz," notes Steve Summers, vocalist for Sprung Monkey. "I opened a magazine at home in San Diego, and I saw a full-page ad. Then there was this total blitz on three powerhouse stations. Now we have a Web site, and someone handling all our mail, and they're sending merchandising out all over. It's all helped us go platinum."

The Web has become a popular new promotion tool because it is, according to Bryn, "the medium that can combine all other media. Like with a magazine, you can refer back to it, it doesn't evaporate like television. Online, you can see it and you can hear it. You can plug into all the different senses on the Internet, but the question with the Internet is still, How do you attract the audience for it?"

## Understanding Evolving Media

Promotion people and media savants who have been working in the business for twenty years have seen many things come along to change the nature of the music marketplace.

"In the old days, you just had the secretary do the publicity; it was never really taken seriously," recalls Mitch.

Along came MTV, video, cable, Internet—if you're not on it, you can get lost in these new mediums.

"I can remember a meeting where the head of a record company said to me, 'This new MTV thing—we're not going to provide them free programming. This will never fly. We are not going to do it,'" chuckles Bryn.

You absolutely can't stop progress, so you might as well dive into it and go with it. Constantly watch for new ways of doing things.

"At least every six months I evaluate everything that my department is doing," insists Bryn. "Just because it worked yesterday doesn't mean it's going to work tomorrow."

When she was at Geffen Records, Bryn noticed that a few entertainment businesses were doing daily faxes promoting their artists. This gave her the idea for Geffen to start its own fax news service. It put out blurbs on the artists on a weekly basis. The purpose was to use the bits of information to get column items and it wasn't a huge time commitment. Geffen was hugely successful with this fax effort. That ran its course after news faxes became a trend and people became numb to them. Once it hits, everybody's on the bandwagon of what the new method is, and it dilutes the effectiveness of the project.

"You dive right into any new medium instantly," insists Laura Cohen, manager of publicity for Virgin Records.

Can you imagine a label not taking advantage of new technology now? That's exactly like people who say, "Oh, new music will never be sent electronically. No one will ever buy them that way. You'll never download an entire album." How can people looking at a five-year historical perspective have head-in-the-mud ideas like that? It boggles your mind, but some people just don't like change.

> **Commit it to memory:** *A good publicist embraces all emerging media. The way to make the most of new technologies is to take advantage of them.*

# The Changing Role of Media, Publicity, and Promotion

In the past couple of decades, publicity has become a lot more important. In this media-intensive time, people in the music business have learned that publicity is not just the packaging and disseminating of information. A great review isn't necessarily what sells a record. It's what you do with that review to support the efforts of sales and promotion, and the quotes that you can flaunt. That's where the real power of publicity is.

"Publicity has become a lot more professional and powerful, and I like to think that I have contributed to that in some small way," admits Bryn. "It was a mission of mine, and it's definitely different now, whether I participated in or just benefited from it."

# A Word about Music Journalism

Music journalists are people who love music and the excitement of the music industry; they have carved out their own way to work with bands. They become specialists by passion, and have very exciting work. They're always going somewhere—on the road, in the studio, to the record company offices, to dinner, and just hanging out with the band. The perks are great, the pay is not. Relatively few music media people make a really good living unless they rise up to the level of producer, director, or editor. Working in the music media is a highly desirable area, so the salaries tend to be lower.

"I started out as a newspaper reporter making only $400 a month," notes Bryn. "I just thought you're never going to make a lot of money as a reporter. Then the head of a public relations firm that specialized in music campaigns convinced me to prostitute myself and go to the other side for $440 a month."

As they're not paid particularly well, music journalists get into the business for the sheer pleasure of it. Their tastes fill a lot of niches—punk, heavy metal, R&B, hip hop, left of center soul music. Unless they find a solid position at a magazine or newspaper, their careers tend to be fairly short. After getting their feet wet, most move on to higher-paying levels. Perhaps one in a dozen rises to prominent positions, such as MTV's Kurt Loder, who came from *Circus* magazine, and Launch.com's Dave DiMartino, who began his career as editor of *Creem* magazine.

"The best way to become a successful journalist, and then perhaps a well-paid one, would be to find a special niche in a given marketplace," confirms Andy Secher, editor of *Hit Parader* and president of Metal, Inc. "If one can find where such an opportunity exists, a little skill and a little knowledge can be parlayed into something significant. Too many young journalists try to be the 'best' in their field and face very rough sledding due to incredible competition. But by creating a path of least resistance, one can actually create a long and successful career."

*chapter 17*

# THE WEB:
## *Draw the Online* 𝄇

The Net changes the balance of power, giving it to the artist, whereas it used to be with the record label. One of the things that's exciting about the Net is we're changing the definition of what breaking an artist means. I think a lot of artists would be happy if they made a living playing the music. They don't have to get filthy rich, but I think they'd like to be able to feed their family, have a nice house, and still play music.

—MICHAEL ROBERTSON, CEO
MP3.COM

The Web offers a myriad of opportunities for virtually everyone in the music business—whether you are a hotshot producer, a publicist, an art director, or a dedicated member of a band who can't get a record contract. The music industry paradigm that has been in place for a generation is changing. The capabilities that the Web provides have made the brick and mortar retail model an impossible one to sustain. Now we have to watch and see how the industry evolves into what will be the virtual marketplace.

"The music business is well situated to realize how much new technology can help it because music has seen that help in the past," declares John Bates, cofounder and evangelist for BIGWORDS.com. "What compact discs did for the music industry was to open it up and make it grow. The World Wide Web is doing the same."

Look at MP3.com, a place for bands to post their music so the public can have access to what they're creating. When MP3.com went public, CEO Michael Robertson became a billionaire.

"At MP3.com, we'll post any artist in the world," says Michael about his site's business philosophy. "They can sell CDs through us. There are no start-up fees, no monthly fees, no binding contracts. We're really offering distribution for artists who do not currently participate in today's music industry system."

Today, there are opportunities that weren't even talked about a year ago. The music industry kept thinking that this wasn't going to happen, but it has. The popularity of pirated music is a good example of how much demand there is for downloadable audio. Now there is a way—besides TV and radio—to help bands reach a wider audience.

"The entire music industry needs to go though some serious introspection and re-engineer its model," notes Al Teller, former chairman/CEO of MCA Music Entertainment Group and founder of AtomicPop.com. "We look at the Web as an enormous tool of empowerment for artists, allowing them to command the lion's share of revenue that comes through this medium. We want to let our artists reach their audience in the most efficient way possible, and we consider MP3 downloads an important part of that."

The Web has the potential to be a positive force for record labels. By their numbers, 85 percent of bands don't break even. The Web can help labels make better choices and perhaps cut down on the unprofitable bands they sign by 50 percent. Think about it: That would have an incredible effect on the bottom line for record labels. The music industry has so much to win.

The traditional record industry has fallen behind the curve, as exemplified by the ill-fated Secure Digital Music Initiative (SDMI). SDMI was the industry's attempt to standardize rights management and licensing for digital content. By the middle of 1999, SDMI had become obsolete, allowing for large loopholes through which Web entrepreneurs could reinvent the system.

"With new technology and new media comes a potential threat to labels and artists," said Ahmet Ertegun, cochairman and co-CEO of the Atlantic Records Group. "But for as long as there has been a music business, people have feared the changes that occur, whether it be 78 records, 45s, cassettes, CDs, and now the Internet. Nothing matters at all if the music isn't there to begin with. Technology is a tool to get the music out there. Be careful not to let the preoccupation with technology interfere with the art."

The music audience is one of the driving forces behind the growth of the Web. In the next couple of years, sale of music on the Internet is expected to become a $3-billion-a-year business. For businesses, the challenge is to connect the real-world audience and the virtual audience, using traditional record company outreach strategies together with the Web.

One artist transcending the traditional marketplace is the always eclectic Robert Fripp, the leader of the veteran British/American band King Crimson. He has formed Discipline Global Mobile (DGM), a company that devises new methods for getting its music heard by those who wish to hear it. Fripp envisions his venture both as an ethical endeavor for musicians and a business opportunity.

"The record companies are becoming increasingly established in the mainstream. Mainstream record companies are focusing in on the mainstream, and they're wafting all around," notes Robert Fripp. "The other thing that's happening is that there's an eruption, mainly supported by technology and artists outside the mainstream."

Fripp, a thirty-five-year veteran of the music industry, formed DGM to create a new artist revenue model.

"As an artist, it was no longer possible for me to work for major labels—there was no way to get around this fact of copyright ownership, which I had always understood to be my property. You can make a case for the royalty rates that the majors pay. You cannot make a case for record companies owning the photographic copyrights," observes Fripp. "The only alternative at that point is to form an independent record label, which is the last thing any player wishes to do."

DGM offers music via a variety of distribution forms, including traditional retail, mail order, and downloading via the Web. DGM also encourages artists to make money by selling albums at gigs. The band can buy their record from DGM in England for five pounds (about $7.50) and sell it for between thirteen and fifteen pounds (around $20) at the show. If they sell ten albums, the act has made eighty pounds ($200); if they sell a hundred, they've made a fair amount of money. It's DGM's way of helping musicians earn a living making music.

"The future that I see is a way for musicians to wrest control of their career from the established recording industry and put it squarely in their own hands," notes Rod Underhill, director of business affairs for MP3.com. "My training in the entertainment area taught me that the most artistic people have the least control. They may have an album rejected by a record company because it didn't have the right flavor or feeling. That sort of thing is troublesome, and I'd hope that we can establish alternatives for musicians who are outside the scope of the traditional recording empire."

## Web Appeal

"Music is a global product," notes Larry Rosen, chairman and CEO of N2K and Music Boulevard/CDNow, a prominent online music vendor located at cdnow.com. "There are no language barriers, people all over the world are into music. And the idea of having a network to link these people together is very, very exciting."

Before the Web, music was only broadcast via TV and radio. You would have a radio station in France, another in China, another in Japan, and one in every city in the United States, but there was little opportunity to broadcast music around the world. The Web provides the necessary infrastructure to build a global music community.

"Ready or not, all of us have to prepare for the implications of the Web as a distribution and delivery channel," noted Tom Freston, MTV Networks chairman. "Whatever happens anywhere will spread like wildfire around the world via the Web. It appears the Web cannot be stopped."

It's a very exciting point in the evolution of humankind. The Web is impacting music consumers, artists, and music companies in four important ways:

1. By providing users with easy access to music with a click of the mouse
2. By allowing consumers to connect with artists and other fans
3. By offering consumers choices of music and formats
4. By fostering creativity by bringing together talent and fans

"The main thing that the Internet will do, though, will be to make music more central to people's lives—make it more important and more accessible," observes Tom Freston. "That is a pretty powerful business opportunity."

With Tom leading the way, MTV has attempted to create the "ultimate online music destination," offering information, community experience, and e-commerce, as well as opportunities for consumers to listen to streaming audio and customize channels by genre. MTV committed $150 million over a five-year period to expand worldwide with localized versions of its Web sites.

> **Commit it to memory:** *The Internet offers a tremendous marketing opportunity, but be advised, profits are made in smaller increments by selling to specialized markets.*

## The Rise of Downloadable Audio Formats

"Downloadable music sites like MP3.com are giving an opportunity to artists who have historically been locked out of the music system," notes

Michael Robertson of MP3.com. "The music industry revolves around the platinum sellers. Acts selling a million CDs or more—that's where the music industry makes its money. Artists who sell less than 5,000 CDs really aren't profitable for the music industry."

What music industry accounting has done is establish a certain dollar value in the musical product of a recording artist. A band may find itself excluded from its contract when it has a relatively large number of fans, but the number of albums that are expected to be sold is so low that the recording company doesn't want to shell out the money to release the next album. This system means the fans are left without any new product and the band is left unemployed.

Supply and demand—a basic economic principle—is at work here. There is a select audience for most types of established music. Profits are made in smaller increments, so for an efficient, streamlined marketing and distribution system, we can create a solid fan base and core marketing opportunity.

"Historically, when an artist could use his artistic endeavors to support himself, you saw better art coming out in those periods in history," notes Mark Mothersbaugh, founder of Mutato Muzika and DEVO. "When people were just indentured servants and were on salary for a king or a pharaoh or a dictator or a corporation, their art was not as expressive."

Rapper Ice-T considered such creative marketing and promotion issues as he was preparing his own online record label, Coroner Records. "It's called that because I see the death of the record companies coming," Ice-T admits. "The Net gives me a chance to help kids sell a few records and make a few bucks."

Change is in the air. The business of the digitization of music is in the early phases of development. Music is being purchased by the unit, just as singles were sold in the sixties, to test the waters. In the next few years, entire albums will be downloaded. Envision this evolution as a five-year process involving multiple steps.

The catalyst for all this Internet audio upheaval has been Moving Picture Expert Group 1 (MPEG-1) Layer 3, or MP3, the much-hyped audio compression format. During the last year or so, MP3 has become the format of choice for the digital music files that now commonly circulate on the Internet. That, in turn, has spawned a growing industry of Web merchants and playback devices catering to the format.

The MP3 format is free and very empowering to the consumer—right now. Tomorrow it may be VQ4. It's an evolving medium, but the market for downloadable audio is not about to shrink.

"It's important to distinguish between MP3 and the MP3 community," observes Jonathan Hahn of the Israel-based copy protection software company MusicMarc. "The format will be replaced but the wants of the people certainly won't."

The record companies fought downloadable audio kicking and screaming, but when they realized that the downloadable audio format was not going to go away just because they objected to it, they quickly struck alliances with the manufacturers of high-profile downloadable audio technology, like the Rio portable music player, Liquid Audio's Liquid Distribution, and Reciprocal.

"A lot of the concerns I hear remind me of what people said about the first VCRs," observes the Offspring's Dexter Holland. "They said that no one would go to see movies when they could stay home and dub them. But that worked itself out. MP3 will help to promote music to more people. If there is one thing that the music companies are good at, it is protecting their stuff. I'm sure that the encryption will fall into place. It really won't be a problem once the industry figures out how to sell stuff on the Internet. It's cool to give away music for free, though . . . that's part of what I think will end up happening."

Much to the chagrin of the major record labels, MP3 files can be freely copied and distributed, with little copyright protection or direct financial gain. The issue is one that record labels are only now coming to terms with.

"The music industry hasn't coped well with MP3 in the past," says Lucas Graves, an analyst at Jupiter Communications in New York. "Now they're shifting from fear and denial to adaptability. They're starting to work with the technology rather than reject it."

## The Problem the Web Has Created for Established Musicians

Freely available software allows music fans to "rip" songs from CDs and compress the music into relatively small digital files that sound almost as good. When the files are created for personal use, the process is legal, according to the 1992 Audio Home Recording Act, but e-mailing a file to another computer user or offering it for download on the Web is not. While such acts of Internet music piracy are common (the Recording Industry Association of America estimates that at least 65,000 illegally offered songs are available on the Web), to date no one has been formally accused of the crime.

"Obviously, bands need to be compensated for their art," notes Megadeth frontman Dave Mustaine. "The record companies need to be a little bit more in tune with the technology of the Web. We have known that this was going to happen for a long time. And I think that basically the music industry was caught with its pants down."

Other artists realize that the Web is not a way to deny them royalties, but a way to augment their body of work, and keep their fan base excited and energized.

"The Internet offers artists a direct marketing tool," asserts Vernon Reid, former frontman for Living Colour. "For example: ways that an artist can bypass the marketing model of record labels and market their work directly; ways artists can be in more immediate communication with their fan base; ways the artist can find new fans; ways the artist can distribute a wider variety of releases in different genres other than those that have mass appeal; ways an artist can distribute work differently."

Multiplatinum Columbia Records act the Offspring has taken a leap into the deep end of digital music space by offering an exclusive track for digital download via the Web. "Beheaded," a song that was originally released on the band's own Nitro Records, can be found on the Web courtesy of a2b Music and RealNetworks.

"We wanted to do something that allowed us to directly interact with our audience," notes Offspring frontman Dexter Holland. "MP3 and the Internet have been a real eye-opener for us . . . it's almost as if it is a new global radio station. We decided to do this after reading that we were the number-one most pirated band on the Internet. We figured this is just a good way to get our music across to kids who want to hear it."

For many established musicians, offering unique, non-album tracks for download is a form of marketing and promotion.

"Putting new audio on the Net is our way of rewarding fans," notes Mark Tremonti, guitarist for the multiplatinum rock group Creed. "We don't do it for profit. We put it on there for free, just so people don't forget about us. It gives people something they can grab onto until our next album comes out."

Creed's Web site, *www.creednet.com,* gets in the neighborhood of 60,000 hits a week. What would those fans be doing if they didn't have Creed's Web site to turn to for information? Probably getting into another band.

"Music sites have graduated from mere marketing vehicles to becoming far-reaching communities where fans and artists come together," confirms MTV's Tom Freston. "The next step—digital delivery of music—is not far behind."

## Where Profits Can Be Found

The Web is like the Wild Wild West: You get out there and you stake your claim. There are dozens of niches for music entrepreneurs to make money on the Web by combining revenue streams from sales, advertising, and subscription.

"Where I think we're going is into the age of a consumption-based model," observes Marc Geiger, cofounder of ARTISTdirect, a triple-faceted entertainment venture. "With the downloading of individual songs and albums, pricing is really the key. It doesn't matter how it gets to you, it matters how much you the consumer are willing to pay for the value you're getting from the music."

If customers will pay $11.99 for an album they bought in a store, they're probably going to laugh in your face if you try to sell them a downloadable album at the same price. Take the *Wall Street Journal* as an example. A paper subscription is $400, but it's only $49 to subscribe online—plus you get more value as an online subscriber.

"I think musicians—even major musicians—will give their product away for free," asserts Rod Underhill, director of business affairs for MP3.com. "That's the future. The future is a Bruce Springsteen–like person not signing his third major label contract. He'll take his music away from traditional distribution and distribute it for free on the Internet, making his money off advertising revenue."

## Bigger, Better, More!

In 1998, .05 percent of all CD sales were online. By 2004, that number is expected to grow by 10–15 percent. There is the potential for more. It's not just about convenience. On the Web it's possible to maintain massive inventory because it's a virtual environment.

"What you're going to see is a lot of specialty products, a lot of live performances," notes Michael Robertson. "A lot of commemorative performances—Princess Di dies; Michael Jordan retires. After those events, you're going to see a commemorative CD come out."

As a Web-only imprint, Rhino Handmade is able to provide limited-edition releases that are otherwise too difficult to find or are out of print. The imprint also posts specific information about each release—such as the release date, audio files, and the pressing limit for a new project—to keep potential buyers up to date on the music that's available.

## Label Executives Embrace the Web

In 1999, the music industry experienced a lot of upheaval. Several record company presidents lost their jobs and reemerged as Web entrepreneurs. Record industry veteran Gary Gersh (who, among other things, was the Big Man at Capitol Records), in conjunction with rock manager John Silva, reentered today's music business with the launch of a Web record company called >EN Music Group. The cybermusic start-up, a subsidiary of Digital Entertainment Network Inc., creates and streams youth-oriented shows on the Web.

"We spent a lot of time chasing money to start our own label, but the longer the process went on, the farther we got from what we really wanted to do," Gersh said. "We wanted to be involved with something small and creative, not something giant and corporate. What appealed to us about >EN was the chance to be part of something bigger than a record company—a twenty-first-century Internet-based media company designed to use music as part of a larger, more exciting whole."

>EN offers artists higher royalty rates and shorter-term contracts that allow acts to retain 50 percent ownership of their master recordings. The company plans to promote, sell, and eventually distribute recordings from >EN's current Web site, which also features dozens of shows about punk rock and extreme sports.

Besides signing their own acts to >EN, Gersh and Silva will look to build sales of other major and independent record companies by loading >EN's original programs with music that viewers can buy while watching the programs. >EN hopes to create new marketing opportunities for its acts and competing bands by creating episodes of original Web video programming starring rock and hip-hop artists, which will cost less to produce than most music videos.

"This isn't like some major label where you have one lone Internet guy off in the corner of this giant machine trying to figure out how to reach the audience on the Internet," Silva said. "These guys understand what Web users want and how to deliver it."

## The Benefits for New Bands

La Junta is a rap group that has risen out of a Chicago 'hood via the Web. When they first started out on MP3.com, their fan base seemed to double every day. Without anything but local promotion, they have over 1,000 downloads and over 3,000 previews.

Why is this relevant? The Web is a means of grabbing attention from specific demographics and enabling a group in an otherwise fringe genre (Hispanic hip hop) to reach its audience. The Web breaks down the otherwise dual class system of superstar/starving artist and creates a wide arena for the middle-class musician.

"I'm making money. Not enough to pay all of the rent, but enough to pay for most of the next CD," notes Jason Rubenstein, who bills himself as a composer/texturalist. "My first CD, *Image,* went into the black after fourteen months, mostly on licensing income. The new CD is still in the red after three months. I think of it as a snowball made of nickels. Pretty soon all those nickels translate into a whole lotta dough."

In his attempt to become a working musician, using the Web as one means of promoting his music, Jason learned not to let the music out for free. "The promotional uses I get are all paid for by use . . . they pay for each 'spot' multiplied by each 'needledrop.' So, for example, if NBC or CBS or someone uses two clips for three spots, I get paid for six uses. For a program or video, it's different. Depending on the distribution and size of the production company and how good it is for my exposure, I may only 'charge' the company for copies of the video, a quote for my press kit, and a list of all retail outlets they send their product to so I can coattail my CD out there. Or, I may charge half price and some of the above, or full rate. I find that the major players will pay full rate if they really like/want/need the music. Chances are they're behind schedule and need it *now*, so they aren't willing to haggle for more than about ten minutes. Frankly, they can afford it, and I can't afford not to charge them."

The Web creates a whole new market that is more regional as well as more specific. Digital distribution creates brand new doors. From a business standpoint, the Web represents:

- Freedom from distribution strangleholds
- Freedom from being dependent on mass media for marketing and promotion
- The ability to communicate directly to your constituency in a two-way fashion

## What the Web Offers the Music Business

"One of the interesting things about the music industry is that it doesn't know who its customers are," Michael Robertson points out. "On the Net, the possibility is there to know your customer and the doors that open up allow the artist to have an ongoing relationship with the customer."

For artists and the people around them to be successful, they need to tap into all the potential revenue streams available to them—not just CD sales, but merchandising, concert sales, promotion, the endorsements. All those aspects are important. And by having a personal, ongoing relationship with their customers, artists can build that kind of loyalty—and generate greater revenues—over time.

Artists who have small followings—those who are just starting out, or those who don't attract a mainstream listening audience—really don't fit into the corporate music system. By contrast, the Web offers both exposure and a new and vast distribution system.

"If it doesn't get heard, it doesn't matter how good it is—you're not going to sell anything," notes Michael Robertson.

The Web will not work effectively as your sole promotional tool; it needs to be synergistically incorporated into other promotions in more traditional forms of media. An easy and efficient way to market a band is to stick your URL on your advertising, put it on your bios, and stick it on the album itself. The Web is another part of the advertising process. Fansrule.com, for example, uses its URL much like a logo on anything it distributes:

"I heard an interesting statistic that 70 percent of CD buyers don't know when the artist that they bought CD number one from comes out with a new CD," notes Michael. "The Net can change that. If you know who bought your first CD, you can tap them on the shoulder and say, 'Hey, I just released my next CD.'"

The Web is a great way to cultivate repeat buyers. After Joe in Des Moines buys a Limp Bizkit record and plays it nine hundred times in nine months, one day he's going to look at the CD cover and notice that URL in the small type and say to himself, 'Wow! They've got a Web site. Holy moly!' Suddenly, a whole new world opens up. Joe downloads a page and finds thirty seconds of a new song from the new album, and then it's the try-it-then-buy-it scenario. Now you've got something that you just don't get from traditional distribution—a repeat buyer. Try-it-then-buy-it is definitely where it's at, repeat buyers are where it's at, and that's part of the twenty-first-century business model for the online artist.

"When you work with the Beastie Boys or Marilyn Manson, those sites get a lot of traffic just by the nature of the size of the artist," observes Marc Geiger. "They're getting 15,000 to 20,000 people a day. On those sites, the commerce portion gets proportionately fewer hits, but they still get 5,000 to 10,000 people looking at a commerce site per day, which is a really healthy number of eyeballs. So the bottom line is just looking in the marketplace and seeing how fast e-commerce is growing. The key to the growth of our Ultimate Band List *(www.UBL.com)* is marketing by us and the key to the growth of the artists' sites is marketing by the artists. Every time artists go on tour and push their domain or Web addresses in multiple forms, that's really where they're going to see spikes in their own traffic and sales."

## The Money Is in Knowing the Consumer

"When we did the Tom Petty promotion, in two days we did 156,000 downloads," notes Michael Robertson. "The real significance of that download was that we now know 156,000 people who like Tom Petty."

The Web makes marketing music easy. When you release a record by an artist, the goal is to have that record become available in every territory of the world, and to promote it and market it on a global basis. Prior to the Web, international promotion and marketing was difficult. People who were big fans of a particular artist in Poland might not hear that the artist had a new record out until three months after its release. Now, you can put that information up on the Web and fans around the world can get information on a new release instantaneously.

"We did a downloadable audio promotion with Buckcherry and it was fabulous because it got people's attention focused on the artist," observes Bryn Bridenthal. "It got people to listen. About 20,000 people downloaded that song: They were the people who had been intrigued, who then might go and plunk down money for the rest of the album. There were people who began to know who Buckcherry was: They had some name identification; we weren't starting at zero."

The Web is one of the most cost-effective ways to do marketing and promotion. You can put something neat up on the Web that has a life of its own for almost nothing, basically the sweat off your brow. Your biggest expense is time. The amount of money you need to produce something compelling on the Web can be the cost of the hardware and software that you need to create it.

"Our Web site lets us do things with community, commerce, and connectivity that allow us to offer our audience news, tidbits, merchandise, sounds, audio files and video files, get into chatting bulletin boards," notes Megadeth's Dave Mustaine. "Not enough artists are aware of the viability and the promotional potential offered by a Web site. I believe that the Internet is one of the most important business tools in marketing and developing a relationship with the audience."

The obvious, immediate benefit of the Web is that it's an easy way to develop a better relationship with potential customers. The Web has become a new marketing tool to appeal to the youth of the world. As far as the way they listen to their music, they're platform agnostic—open to new experiences. Plus, it's a great way to develop a captive audience. Established artists—like Tom Petty—have already realized that they have enormous things to gain from the Web as well.

## Big Money

Perhaps the best person to comment on the Web's moneymaking ability is Michael Robertson, founder of MP3.com. When the company went public in July 1999, Michael owned nearly 26 million shares of his company. It was a good IPO. Stock prices began at $28 and closed in the $60-a-share range in the first day of trading.

"With all artists, it's important to focus on revenue potential, not just CD sales but concert tickets, merchandising, etc.," notes Michael. "The Net changes some economic principles of the process. For example, when Universal merged with Polygram, two major record labels came together, and it's pretty well known that they dropped a bunch of acts. It's thought that 200,000 was the cutoff—if you sold less than 200,000 CDs, you got dropped. But at 200,000 CDs, the reality is that artists made no money for themselves.

"But you take those same artists, and you put them on the Net. And let's say they sell 40,000 CDs, or only one-fifth of what they did at traditional retail. However, instead of selling their CDs for $16.99, which they traditionally cost in the U.S., you sell them for $10—a notable price decrease—but, the artists get half the money off the top, which is a significantly higher percentage than they make at a record company."

Those same artists who made no money for themselves or their record label by selling 200,000 CDs, could move to the Web, sell 40,000 CDs at $10 each, make $5 per CD, and gross $200,000 a year selling albums. One of the real potentials of the Web is that it's so direct. It really changes the underlying economic dynamics. Now, artists have the opportunity to enjoy much greater splits of the revenue than they traditionally have ever seen before.

## The Future

Going forward, we're going to see a lot of new business models in the music industry. The only business model that we know today is the CD-selling model. It's a model of scarcity. You don't get any music until you give up $16—that's the model. The model we see on TV works differently: The more people who hear a song on TV, the more money the act makes and the more money the TV channel makes. With music, you might see ads incorporated into songs—actual product placement within a song. Imagine a song that mentions Diet Pepsi or Chevrolet or Kentucky Fried Chicken. Some artists might say that's heresy, but that's probably one of the models that will emerge in this century.

"I've had a bit of luck getting onto the local radio shows. Here's how: Try and write songs that pertain to your area's market . . . like Jimmy Buffet wrote island type, ocean stuff . . . the Keys' radio stations love it!" notes songwriter David S. Kennedy, Sr., whose music can be found at *www.wserv.com/~dkennedy.* "Write Key West tunes if you're in the Florida area. If it's good, they'll be glad to play it. If you live in Southern California, then write beach songs and take them to the local radio shows . . . I wonder who may have done that? Find the niche and local radio will play it."

## Buy a Subscription

You may also see some subscription models, à la cable TV. Pay $20 a month, get any song you want, any time you want, any way you want. Maybe that will transform the CD collection into a service, where it's not about collecting CDs—it's about subscribing to this service and having everything streamed on demand.

Online music is still in its infancy. You can't look at that baby and say, "What can it do? I know other humans. They can run and shoot basketballs and count and read. What can a baby do? This baby can't do anything." What we have here is an immature medium. It's just been born and it's going to take a while for that newborn to grow and mature and learn. It's a little premature to measure it and give the baby an IQ test.

# Section iii

## Paths for Musicians: The Long and Winding Road

# MAKING MUSIC FOR A LIVING:
## *Further on Up the Road* 𝄇

Music has given me over forty years of extraordinary experiences. I can't say that life's pains or more tragic episodes have
been diminished because of it. But it's allowed me so many
moments of companionship when I've been lonely and a sub-
lime means of communication when I wanted to touch people. It's both my doorway of perception and the house that I
live in.

—DAVID BOWIE, SINGER/SONGWRITER, VISIONARY

## Moving Along

*T*wenty years ago, when you were just getting into the music business, you probably weren't thinking about where you would be in
the year 2000. If you were in a punk or new wave band, you were
of the mindset that there was no future, and you lived for the day.
When someone first talked to you about evergreen financial situations like
publishing, the thought of building up a catalog—so you could buy, sell,
and trade your music for years to come—was of no interest. You were
young, on the road, paying the bills by making music.

The music business is a fluid, cyclical business. You are never what
you once were. You switch labels, bands, management companies, promoters—relatively few people who are not running their own companies
are doing the same job they were a decade ago.

"I'm a producer now, I'm at a different part of my life," notes JJ
French. "Back when I was twenty-five, I wanted to be playing on an album

and going out on tour. My focus is not to be the live performer anymore; now I enjoy producing. I imagine I could wind up as a record executive."

When a band is just starting out in the working world, they are expected to sacrifice normal comforts like home and family to become rock stars. You won't have a stable relationship with your significant other because your band is always the priority. Your family relations are tough because you're on tour for Thanksgiving, the Fourth of July, Easter, and Christmas. Some relationships make it; some don't. If you haven't yet reached arena popularity, there comes a time—usually when you get to be around thirty—when you abandon your aspirations of being a megastar and settle into a comfortable position in the music business.

"You want to know what made me leave a band situation—tuna fish," declares Vince Castellucci of the Harry Fox Agency. "Everybody should think about what they're going to do in the future. How am I going to pay the bills? Where do I want to go? Do I always want to do the work of being my own roadie, my own musician? Do I really want to work with a superstar and have to play that game? Do I want to be outside the media's radar scope?"

After seven and a half years on the road, Vince decided to make a change to a more stable situation where he could come home every night, but still work in the music industry. Even after life on the road, the music industry can be very exciting for a lot of reasons. You don't have to do as much physical work, so it lets you slow down a bit. You don't have to lose your chops, but you can still take it easy at night more often. You will also gain a broader understanding of how the music industry operates—from writer to musician to recording artist to how you get the product out.

"Once the product is out to when you get the bottom line back in your bank account is a very interesting process," notes Vince. "A lot of people like to make it seem like a very complicated mystery. It's not. You have a piece of product that's for sale. They get paid and you get paid. That's the way it's supposed to work, but it doesn't really work that way."

## We All Change

Being musical and getting old in the music business doesn't mean you're a has-been; it just means that your rock star days are past and now you can have something closer to a normal life.

"As I get older, I still get off on the playing side of it, but the endless running around—basically the other twenty-two hours of the day—are less and less effortless," notes Lars Ulrich of Metallica. "It used to be effortless for me to travel; it never used to bother me. The last few years, it's become more of an effort for me to travel. That's probably got something to do with getting older."

As artists age in the music business, they can also do things that they wouldn't have been able to do as younger, less established entities. If Metallica had not sold more than 30 million albums worldwide, there would have been precious little chance that Lars Ulrich, James Hetfield, Kirk Hammett, and Jason Newsted would have appeared onstage playing heavy metal accompanied by the San Francisco Symphony.

"When I was a young man, I was caught up in the Beatles and pop music and being a young hipster," confirms Matthew Wilder, cocomposer for the movie *Mulan*. "But I grew up on Broadway. My father was a theatrical adviser, so I saw the original cast of *Oliver* and *The Sound of Music*. I had a real love for that grandeur, but it wasn't until I matured that I was capable of tackling something as big and sweeping as a Disney film. A lot of musicians tend to be pigeonholed early on in their careers. There were many things I wanted to do, but getting there was 90 percent of the job."

## Defining Success

To earn a living making music, you need to ask yourself: What defines a successful musician? Sounds weird, but you should be clear on your objectives. Success means different things to different people at different points in their lives.

Remember the kids you knew who played in wedding bands back when you were teenagers? They thought they'd end up being the Rolling Stones. At some point in their lives, they changed their focus. They certainly didn't say, "I want to wind up in a wedding band." But they wound up in a wedding band, and it was obvious that they weren't going to be the Beatles or anybody else, and they still love to play. Not everybody can be a star; not everybody can become famous. You need to figure out what success means to you.

"As far as when I felt successful, on different levels, I felt successful when I was in Akron, Ohio, and wrote early DEVO songs with the other guys," recalls Mark Mothersbaugh, whose work ranges from cofounding new wave icons DEVO to writing music for *The Rugrats*. "Success on another level was the idea of getting a record deal and getting your music played by other people. We weren't sure how successful we could ever be on a commercial level because we came from a different aesthetic than Sting and Van Halen. We liked Andy Warhol's method of looking at the world and interpreting what he saw around him. He was an artistic reporter, and that appealed to us. Music was very self-satisfying, but then you say, What's the bigger challenge? If you can turn other people on, that's a great thing."

# Making Music for a Living

"If you can do something that makes people happy, there's nothing better," notes JJ French. "I get thank-you's from people all the time who say, 'Thank you for Twisted Sister . . . You were so great and you meant so much.' That makes me so happy."

If the music makes you happy, then you've succeeded. It's certainly not the gold and platinum record or the money. If you watch MTV's *Behind the Music,* it's the same story every week—drugs, sex, alcohol, ripped-off managers. It's just one horror story after another—so money isn't it.

"The music business is not a static business. You're either going up or you're going down. For people with bipolar disorders, it's terrifying," observes JJ French. "You can't just go on with this thing, The audience loves me today and doesn't love me tomorrow. It will destroy you."

David Javelosa has been all over the music business. Back in the seventies, his band, Los Microwaves, had a major label distribution deal. He got a degree in electronic music from Cal Arts and composed and produced an opera. Technology always was part of his music, and he realized where there's technology in the music biz, and that there was money to be made there. So he started composing music for video games.

"It became a comfortable day job, a backup skill. I felt very comfortable mixing the two and it's been lucrative."

These days David calls himself a "composer, producer, currently functioning as a contract technology evangelist for Yamaha, specializing in game developer relations." His life is all about music and sound design. His days consist of composing and arranging music in MIDI and digital audio for game platforms such as the Nintendo 64 and Sony PlayStation as well as for the Web.

"Essentially, my position with Yamaha has me checking their technology—which is hardware *and* software—seeing what works and discovering little pockets of value that further their sales and technology."

Sounds kind of geeky, but did you know that more than 60 percent of computer geeks are musical? There's a genetic link in there somewhere. Most of the work staff at Yamaha are hybrids—musical and technical.

"Everyone seems to be able to write a tune," notes David. "A lot of people go from implementation to full-out programming."

David's pleased with his career direction. "A lot of my game music is commercially oriented: It demands that I make a satisfying amount of original music in that genre. I may end up doing a lot of rearrangement of other music, which is good for my musical chops, and it's satisfying work because I'm not creatively committed to the work and still I make a day's wage out of it."

There are all kinds of successful musicians. If you were the one who would practice all night long, you might end up with a keyboard rig playing jazz in a bar in Las Vegas all night long.

"A successful musician is somebody who is not waiting tables," engineer Bob Rice points out. "I mostly help other people make music, but I've been practicing for years, and I think I'll have an opportunity to do some more playing and performing."

## Staying Humble

No matter how successful you are, it's important to stay humble. Keith Richards, cofounder of the Rolling Stones, doesn't believe he writes any music: "They're floating in the air and they just channel through me out of my fingers to become a melody."

Unless you are the Rolling Stones, it really doesn't matter how big you once were: There's always someone who's going to come along and be more popular—then you become yesterday's news. Be nice to people on the way up, because you're going to see them again on the way down.

Will Smith, also known as the Fresh Prince, and his partner in musical crime, DJ Jazzy Jeff, had just won their first Grammy awards and they were thrilled. After hanging out in Los Angeles, soaking up the sun and savoring their win, the duo hopped a plane back to Philadelphia, their hometown. Everyone met them at the airport and made a huge fuss over them. The mayor even turned out for their arrival. The two took a limo home, where Jeff's mom had made an elaborate celebration dinner.

When Will and Jeff walked into the house, they were walking tall. They were struttin'. The two were feeling pretty important. Jeff's mom congratulated them. Then she asked Will and Jeff to go to the store and buy her a can of yams, a loaf of bread, and a gallon of milk. Will was surprised. He figured that since they were so important now, they wouldn't have to do things like go to the store. But Jeff's mom made them go. She didn't care if they were big stars. She needed her yams.

Will, god of rap music and big and small screens, says he still shops for Jeff's mom, and that that incident really taught him a lesson: Never get the feeling that you are too important to do the little things for the people who matter.

## Continuing in Music

Clearly, artists with established careers become brands. The ones who have longevity are the ones who have the best brand recognition, and have the best brand cachet; if you can retain name recognition more than a decade after your heyday, then you can continue playing live and drawing crowds.

"At this point in my career, it's more important for me to have artistic credibility," notes solo artist Duff McKagan, former bass player for Guns N' Roses. "I never compromised to be hip. I was in punk rock bands at the wrong time. When Guns N' Roses started, it was not hip. Money has never driven me. When I was leaving Gun N' Roses, I was getting Axl Rose calling, saying things like, 'Duff, you're the only one who can save this band.' These carrots were being dangled in front of me . . . it was all money—millions of dollars here and millions of dollars there. That stuff would all go into my head, but it was like, Yeah, but the record we would make would be a killer. Then, one morning I woke up and realized, Wow, this is about the money. I thought, wait a minute, I have a house; I have a car. More than that, it's never been about the money, so why is it now? And I realized, this is not the direction that I want to go. Peace. Guns N' Roses was my college and I learned a lot, but I'm not going to hang out around the campus and work in the campus store. It was a great learning experience, and now I'm moving on."

## Live Versus Studio

When musicians leave the spotlight, they go in different directions. Some, like Duff, keep up the live performances and continue to play clubs. Others, like Duff's former bandmate Slash, go into the studio.

"Live and the studio are two separate experiences," continues Duff. "The studio is an extension of the compositional process. You're building components for a production. Performing live is more of a catharsis, more of an enriching experience for me and, hopefully, for the audience as well. My performances tend to be largely improvisational and more about the experience than a statement promoting a body of work."

Whichever way you go, the ultimate goal is to share your music with others.

"Inevitably, all music has to be participated in by others—whether it's an interactive audience controlling the music in a game or an ensemble that is saddled with the task of reading the score and improvising on it," notes composer David Javelosa. "Of course, the best thing is jamming with musicians who have the same mindset, who are on the same page, who have that nonverbal communication ability. That's the best."

David's goal is simple: to make enough money to make music. "I look at my current position in the hardware industry as a means of developing enough equity to have my own studio, and continuing on with bigger, high-profile projects. Perhaps continuing with a project management score or a game that I'm not really into that they would like me to have participation in. Also I'm starting to subcontract off sound design, some instrument design."

# Playing with Instruments

Some people maintain their connection with music by playing instruments. These include the tour technicians discussed in Chapter 11, in addition to people who support, sell, and repair equipment.

"The music business was not good to me. I had been involved with record companies, I had been involved with artists who wanted to take credit for things that I wrote," notes Ken Rich, founder of Rich Sounds, a keyboard repair and restoration firm. "I had always been involved in repair work, and I finally decided that if I wasn't going to be on stage, I didn't want the musician going on stage without my help."

Vic Firth, the timpani player with the Boston Symphony, has built a business making drumsticks. He started making drumsticks for his students thirty-five years ago; now he has a factory that churns out 80,000 pairs a week.

"I made them for myself, then people started asking for them," he said. "I never envisioned anything of this magnitude."

This business started after Vic Firth became the timpanist for the Boston Symphony in 1952. Firth was dissatisfied with the warped utensils that passed for drumsticks, so he started making his own.

"Anything I've ever done, if it wasn't fun, I didn't do it," Firth said.

His students at the New England Conservatory learned of the sticks and started asking for them. Firth hired a Canadian woodworker to handcraft the sticks he had designed in lots of twenty-five at a time. He took the finished product and burned his name on them by hand.

These days, production takes place at a 65,000-square-foot plant in Newport, Rhode Island, that now employs ninety-seven people. There, wood is dried in kilns to reduce the wood's moisture content and reduce warping before being ground down into sticks and nonmusical items like pepper mills. Quality control standards are high for 200 models of sticks, brushes, and mallets.

Sticks that pass muster are sorted by weight and then tested for pitch, density, flex, and moisture content, using a computer that ensures they're matched perfectly. Firth jokes that any stick with imperfections ends up in his fireplace.

"I bet no drummer out there knows how much that stick goes through to make it to them," says Carole Norton, who is part of a team that stamps Firth's name on 13,500 sticks a shift.

Firth's sticks have captured 40 percent of a market in which there are a dozen competitors, including Pro-Mark, Zildjian, and Regal Tip. Annual sales stand at about $10.5 million.

Firth is in an enviable position because his product, like guitar strings, is not affected by the ups and downs of the economy. Drummers can delay buying a new drum kit and guitarists can delay buying a new guitar, but they must replace broken sticks and strings. Firth's sticks carry a list price of about $10.50 a pair.

"Drumsticks are much like razor blades. You've got to constantly replace them," notes Firth. "If you convince someone to try your product, you have a customer for life."

"There's a lot of stability in what I do because people always need their equipment repaired," confirms Ken Rich.

# WORKING FOR HIRE:

## *Get Out There*

There are a lot of good things about doing music for TV, and some bad. People don't really pay attention to who the composer is on a TV show. Like, you probably don't know who the composer is for *The X-Files*. You don't get the fame jolt, but it gives you a relatively safe place to experiment and hone your craft and take chances . . . so it's kind of a fun medium.

—MARK MOTHERSBAUGH, COMPOSER FOR *THE RUGRATS*
COFOUNDER OF DEVO

## Music in the Air

*T*hink about it: Virtually everything in life has a soundtrack. There's music to accompany you while you're shopping, when you're in a lobby—music for anything you watch on a screen. Somebody's getting paid to make all that music, and it could be you. All it takes is ingenuity and perseverance.

"There is no formula for it. If there were a formula, everyone would do it," advises TV composer Jonathan Wolff, who has composed soundtracks for such primetime shows as *Seinfeld* and *Married . . . with Children*.

Engineer Bob Rice has a long and varied résumé. "I do synthesizer programming, studio wiring, consulting on room layout. I do recording engineering, CD mastering, I've done digital audio editing for multimedia, I've done sound effects design, I've done dialogue editing. I've done multimedia and editing for *Chicago Hope* and *NYPD Blue* at a post house."

He goes out and finds his clients, just as you need to do. Succeeding in any business venture goes back to the same things we've been talking about throughout this entire book: relationships and networking.

If you're into a long-term music career, you should already know some people. What happened to that assistant at Atlantic Records you knew? Perhaps he's become VP of video sales. What about the guys you toured with? Bet they're up to some interesting things. Musicians always need help on projects—perhaps they could use your help. Be creative. Draw on your contacts. You almost certainly know somebody who needs music for something.

Take Tom Viscount, a guy with an album and a band—Viscount. Tom's a sharp talker, and was able to convince someone at Sears to use one of Viscount's songs for a national teen model search. The tune played in the Sears department store chain for five months—how cool is that?

Viscount made about $6,000 off that deal; as a result, they were able to pay back some of the money people lent them to record the album *My Name Is Nobody.*

Another great promotion Tom came up with was to use Viscount's music in conjunction with his day gig with the American Red Cross. He got the Red Cross to use another one of his songs as the theme tune for one of their blood drives. A few more songs and *My Name Is Nobody* will become a greatest hits album.

"I worked out those deals just by knowing people, networking, finding out that there was a need, and submitting the music," shares Tom. "Even if you can get one of your songs in a small movie that doesn't pay much, it gives you exposure."

When a new song by a duo called Melky Sedeck first hit the radio, shoppers at the Contempo Casuals and Wet Seal apparel chains had been hearing the debut single for more than a month. MCA Records, the label behind the duo, made the song available to the stores in advance.

"If someone hears a song in the store, that's an early impression" that can juice up a radio debut, says Paul Orescan, vice president and marketing director for MCA.

Increasingly, recording executives are launching songs or artists in the aisles of specialty apparel stores. Shoppers there tend to be young, fashion-conscious—and some of the biggest music buyers. Most retailers play any one song about three times a day for at least a month in every store in their chain.

Nudging the trend: It's harder than ever to get new music onto major radio stations, which demand proof of audience appeal even for well-known singers. Unknown artists are a tougher sell. So in recent years, record companies have turned to restaurants, coffee shops, and even airlines as outlets to introduce new music.

To reach this audience, record companies don't take music directly to stores. Instead, they send new releases free of charge to music-programming companies that work for retailers, sometimes along with information about an artist's target audience. Programmers match songs—new and old—to stores, based on demographics and a chain's desired image. Programmers won't divulge specific fees for their service, but AEI Music Network Inc., based in Seattle, says it generally charges retailers less than $100 a month for each location that uses its programs. The charge covers licensing and copyright fees.

Executives at the three leading programming companies—AEI Music, Muzak LLC, and DMX LLC—say it isn't their job to introduce new music, but some individual programmers concede that they often get a push from record labels to pair new songs with the hottest stores.

## Volunteering Your Time

If you don't like your contact base, volunteer your time. Benefit shows are a great way to meet important people.

"I've done mixing at benefit shows, and out of that work I've worked with Brian Wilson and Van Dyke Parks, T-Bone Burnett and Jackson Browne, Sam Phillips and Rickie Lee Jones and Stan Ridgway," notes Bob Rice. "Just through going to do benefits, for signing up for the right gigs. I worked my butt off on those days, but they were magical shows."

Find out what's going on in your community. If there's anything happening that's a worthwhile cause—one you won't mind giving up a day of work to do—go for it. And remember: Nothing is really for free. Look at it as an opportunity.

> **Commit it to memory:** *Volunteering for something that advances your career is not working for free. It's an opportunity to meet the right people.*

Marketing a person—yourself—is just like marketing a product. You have to give away the baseball caps and the T-shirts in order to pique people's interest enough to pay attention to you; in the process of doing those benefit shows, you'll develop some key relationships.

"Through benefits, I developed a relationship with a string arranger and a film composer. He's a central figure in the California music scene, so by my doing these benefits, he got to know who I was," explains Bob. "When he was putting together a studio, I helped him buy equipment and get everything set up with the right acoustics. To a guy who's on a film-scoring deadline, fast is everything. That got me working on the film score with him, which is probably the best thing I've ever worked on, and that was from doing volunteer work."

**Commit it to memory:** *Get your work out there and the rest will come.*

## Specialize

If you're looking to make a career doing something other than playing in bands, you'll need to specialize. Do you want to do music for airports? Video games? TV? Movies? The options are endless—just figure out where you want to go and go there. David Javelosa, remember, is a composer, producer, and current technology evangelist for Yamaha, specializing in game developer relations.

David earns a formidable living making music for various projects.

"Working freelance, I secure gigs for both music and sound design," he states. "I compose and/or arrange, generally in MIDI, sometimes in Digital Audio—mostly in both. I deliver audio for game platforms such as Nintendo 64, Sony Play Station, and the Internet."

His coworkers are mostly a hybrid of music and technology people as well. "Everyone seems to be able to write a tune, a lot of people go from implementation to full out programming," he offers.

He's been on the road and is now looking for a quieter life. Working as a game designer is a very comfortable position for him at this point in his career.

"I feel satisfied with my musical statement," David admits.

David Bowie is also making music for video games these days. The Thin White Duke teamed with longtime guitarist and collaborator Reeves Gabrels on *Omikron: The Nomad Soul,* an action-adventure CD-ROM game. Bowie and Gabrels worked with game developers to create original music for *Omikron,* including eight new songs that are exclusive to the game. A virtual CD featuring the songs and music can be purchased in the game by players and taken back to play in their virtual apartment.

"I moved right away from the stereotypical industrial game music sound," Bowie says. "My priority in writing music for *Omikron* was to give it an emotional subtext."

## What You Need to Get a Gig

We all know how David Bowie got his gig, but for those without multi-platinum reputations, you've got to have a set of skills that are in demand.

A musician can find freelance and work-for-hire projects by the following routes:

- By developing a reputation as someone who does something unique or exceptional
- By maintaining a high profile in one's particular area
- By cold-calling contacts, specifically the producers and managers responsible for hiring musicians

You can generate contacts for freelance and work-for-hire projects at trade shows, conferences, seminars, and on other jobs. Basically, networking is what it takes. Eventually, you'll develop a growing list of regular clients, periodically keeping in contact with them or "servicing" them to meet their needs.

## Work-for-Hire Projects

Getting a work-for-hire assignment is really a tradeoff. As a freelancer, you are hired to help out on a onetime basis and then retain the rights to what you create for the job. By contrast, when you create a work for hire, you give up the rights to the music in exchange for greater name exposure and invaluable contacts.

There are plenty of different work-for-hire scenarios—TV shows and jingles for radio, television commercials, video games, and industrial films. The possibilities are limitless. Find a couple of friends who are directors; if they're busy, they need music made.

Getting work for hire is all about developing a reputation. David Javelosa developed his reputation by being one of the first ones doing video games—early adapters are always in a good position. David added value to his position by speaking on trade show panels, joining trade organizations, making connections, taking the jobs, doing people favors, and doing good work.

TV composer Jonathan Wolff had developed a comfortable niche writing easy-to-move-to material for shows such as *Fantasy Island*.

"Often when they needed a song written or a dance routine, a production number—that's what I did," Jonathan confirms.

The who-you-know factor came into play, and voilà—Jonathan went from doing specialized material to writing the theme music for *Seinfeld*—all because of a comedian named George Wallace. Jonathan used to tour with Tom Jones and Diana Ross as their band conductor. George was the opening act. Comedians are friends with each other: George and Jerry Seinfeld happened to be great friends.

"George mentioned to me that his buddy Jerry Seinfeld was trying to get this show going and he was having trouble with music," recalls Jonathan. "They kept talking to composers and hearing music that they didn't like. They weren't sure what to do, so George hooked me up with Jerry. He said to me, 'You're gonna get this call from Jerry. Be nice to him.'

"Jerry called me directly and said 'George Wallace said you're my man,' and showed me what some other composers had tried for him. I recognized that it wasn't a musical problem, but rather a sound design problem. Jerry wanted music that was signature and unique and quirky—identifiable. Remember, this was the late eighties; signature, identifiable TV music meant melody. Thematic melody."

Jonathan recognized the problem: Although the current stylistic trend was to do TV show theme songs with melody, you can't have melody when your lead character is trying to do a monologue. Those two imperatives butt heads. Jonathan approached this sound design problem by taking the melody of the opening title—it's Jerry!

"I built the music around him," shares Jonathan. "Instead of using standard instruments, like drums and clarinets, because of the human nature of the melody—his voice—I went with the organic sounds of the finger snaps, mouth pops, lip smacks, and tongue noises."

In its eight-year run, *Seinfeld* grew to be one of the most successful television series ever, anchoring NBC's Thursday night lineup from 1993 to 1998. The show led NBC into number-one position and to record-making profits of more than $200 million a year—or nearly $1 billion during the first run of *Seinfeld*. Advertisers paid $500,000 or more for each thirty-second commercial spot on the program. The success made Jonathan Wolff a hero.

The exposure he got from writing the *Seinfeld* theme song was a turning point for Jonathan's career. Since then, he's been asked to write theme songs for TV shows like *Caroline in the City, Married . . . with Children, Who's the Boss,* and *Will & Grace,* among others. He says he owes his buddy George Wallace a small island somewhere and an airline to get him back and forth for making the connection with *Seinfeld.*

## Location, Location, Location

Yeah, we know, you don't live in Los Angeles or a major media mecca, so what should you do? Deciding what part of the country to live in depends on the kind of outlet you want to be making music for. Hey, it may just be as the house musician at the local hockey rink whose job is to get the audience excited. Then again, if you're in a big city, it may be something far more interesting, like TV or film composition. It all depends.

If you're going to be one of those people who becomes successful beyond their wildest dreams, you're probably going to end up moving to a major entertainment center like London, New York, Los Angeles, or Tokyo.

"I felt successful when I was in Akron, Ohio, and wrote early DEVO songs with the other guys," recalls Mark Mothersbaugh, cofounder of DEVO and now president of Mutato Muzika—an L.A.–based music production company. "We decided to leave Akron because we wanted to put our aesthetic to the acid test and see if we could sync up with the commercial world, and actually have a life in the world of music."

## The Mother Load

Mark Mothersbaugh is smart—scary smart. You can tell by the way he looks at you, he knows more than you. But you also know he can relate to you—or at least his music can. In his nearly twenty-plus years of making music for public consumption, his work has been repeatedly hailed and honored. In addition to his de-evolutionary work with DEVO and compositions for *The Rugrats,* he has composed for *Pee-Wee's Playhouse;* done work on ads for Miller Lite, Universal Studios, and Toyota; and written compositions for the films *Rugrats: The Movie, 200 Cigarettes,* and *Rushmore.*

"DEVO as a band was part of something bigger—we were actually visual artists first," observes Mark. "We liked the medium of pop art because people like Andy Warhol could work in film, he could work in photography, you could work in fashion or oil paints or silk-screening or you could produce bands—but essentially what our pop art movement was about was solving problems."

Traveling in performance art circles, Mark met interesting people, one of whom was a comic named Paul Rubens, also known as Pee-Wee Herman—a funny, geeky guy. In the early eighties, Pee-Wee had a stage show at the Roxy in L.A. In 1985, he got to do a movie, *Pee-Wee's Big Adventure,* which was a huge success. Pee-Wee's smart, androgynous, quirky comedy was fun for both kids and adults.

Twice Pee-Wee asked Mark to write music for his little production, but DEVO was always out on tour. When Pee-Wee got the TV show, he asked Mark again. DEVOmania was on the decline, and Mark started writing music for the show.

"It was an easy way to get in because they didn't know what they were doing either," recalls Mark. "I wrote extreme music for the different vignettes, and got to create a style for that show. That was the beginning. *Pee-Wee's Playhouse* had some critical success, so it led to other jobs, and to me it wasn't at odds with what DEVO was about at all."

"For me, it was a nice way to feel good about working in the entertainment industry again. When you get into popular music, it's like a nasty septic tank. It's exciting, but it's nasty. It does deplete your own spirit and your own energy."

Mark's highly praised and unquestionably quirky approach to *Pee-Wee's Playhouse* led to other gigs, like commercials, so he started his company—Mutato Muzika—to keep track of everything.

The first commercials Mark did for products by Toyota and Miller Lite won awards. Hollywood loves a winner, so the work kept on coming. Disney asked Mark to write four hundred songs for the TV show *Adventures in Wonderland* in a year and a half.

"When Disney asked, I said, 'I can't do that.'"

"And they said, 'Do you have some friends who want to work with you?'"

"I thought of people who couldn't even walk onto the lot at Disney without security stopping them, but they were very talented artists. I wanted to give those people a vehicle, a chance to interact with the world of entertainment, the world of TV and film. We did songs with a wide range of people, including Billy Mummy, the little guy from *Lost in Space.* He was a great songwriter, and he and his partner Robert wrote many songs for the show."

Today, Mutato Muzika thrives, following on a DEVO vision as a musical cooperative. Bob 1 and Bob 2 from DEVO are at Mutato every day, along with Mark.

"We see it as life after rock 'n' roll, a continuation of what we were doing in a really healthy way because we get offered all of these odd, interesting jobs that have different demands."

## Music for TV

Did you know that more than four hundred series, specials, and made-for-TV movies may be in production during any given week? Making music for TV is a great gig, if you can get it. The money is good and lots of people hear your work, even though there's not much in the way of recognition.

It's rare to find people in the entertainment business who really respect music on television. They're all looking for a deal. If somebody will do it for $20 cheaper, that gets their attention.

In large part, this is due to the way television shows are made. A TV show is assigned a budget; then the producer has to figure out how to make it work. Different amounts are carved out for different responsibilities. The music usually comes at the end of the line.

By the time a TV show gets around to arranging for music, the show has usually exceeded both its time allotment and its budget. So when it comes time to make the music, the producers just want it done. Once the music is in, everyone can get paid.

"It's really stressful," confirms Bob Rice. "Often, there's not enough time to do things to reach the level of quality you're used to because you have to move it through."

The good side of making music for TV is that you get a lot of creative freedom because people don't really care. Do you know who wrote the soundtrack for your favorite television show? Probably not. TV music lets you experiment, hone your craft, and take chances in relative anonymity.

## Movie Music

Film is a much rougher medium for music. There's more of a critical review of all aspects of a film than there is in TV shows, and only about five hundred films are made each year. The great thing about movie music is that whether the score is dramatic, soothing, romantic, comedic, or foreboding, it is an integral part of the fabric of any motion picture. It's also an area where there is opportunity. And if you win the cosmic lottery and have a hit movie with a hit soundtrack, you'll realize that a single song or background score can generate a lifetime of substantial earnings. Not to mention that the creative opportunities that await you are awesome.

"One of the more obvious differences between TV and movies is budget. With the *Rugrats* movie I had a ninety-six–piece orchestra," shares Mark Mothersbaugh. "I like working with directors. I like working with people to help their vision become real."

Movies also offer a captive audience, seated and ready to absorb your music as they watch the film. But remember: The audio goes hand in hand with the video.

"A film composer who wants the full attention of his audience is making a mistake," says John Williams, composer for such films as *Star Wars Episode I: The Phantom Menace.* "It's a minor miracle if it has a life of its own. We're writing music that people are unaware of. You can only compose what the film will tolerate. You can only write what the film will accept. One thinks of serving the film."

Writing for film requires the ability to write different kinds of music. The background score plays under the dialogue, in chase scenes, in romantic settings—it creates or sets the mood, underscoring the action. This is the primary music in most films. Songs are used as visual vocals (a character singing on camera), as visual instrumentals (an orchestra playing on camera), as background music (the Burt Bacharach and Hal David classic "Raindrops Keep Falling on My Head" as Paul Newman and Katherine Ross ride a bicycle in *Butch Cassidy and the Sundance Kid*), or as the opening or closing theme to the film (ZZ Top's "Doubleback" for *Back to the Future III*).

Most successful motion pictures use hit songs to create a period flavor, establish a mood, give an actor a chance to sing, make people laugh, make people cry, and create interest in the movie through successful soundtrack albums and hit singles. Music is also important from a financial point of view. Soundtracks are part of the marketing game in movies.

Make sure you've got some experience when you get into making movie music, since it's not an easy job.

"It wasn't until I matured that I was capable of tackling something as big and sweeping as a Disney film," notes Matthew Wilder.

## Money for Movie Music

If you're going to do music for films, you need to know about the music budget—it's flexible. In the past, the music budget was usually a specific percentage of the total cost of the picture. Now, there is no typical formula. The total music budget really depends on what role music plays in the film and what price tag the producers are willing to pay to achieve what they want the music to accomplish.

Certain films contain only a background score, whereas others combine a background score with new songs and preexisting songs. If it's a big-budget major motion picture, the music budget can range from $150,000 to over $1 million depending on:

- The stature of the background composer
- The type of score required (i.e., orchestra, synthesizer, Dixieland jazz band, etc.)
- The number of preexisting and new songs being used
- The producer or director's commitment to the role and purpose of the music in the overall project

## Giving to Get Back

When you're selling your music for a project and want to retain the rights, avoid entering into a work-for-hire contract. Sell the song, but try not to be commissioned to write it. If you're commissioned to write a song, then it's a work-for-hire situation and you will lose the rights to it. For instance, if Fox Television hires you to write the theme song for its *Lost Universe* TV series, Fox Television (the corporation) becomes the owner of the work, and the person hired to write it (you) disappears from the profit scenario. You'll still get credit for writing the song, but you just won't see any back-end money.

"Twenty years ago, as I did my little negotiation meetings with BMI, and Bobby Weinstein signed over my first publishing advance, he said, 'You've got a body of work here. What you should think about doing is building up your catalog so you can buy, sell and trade stuff,'" recalls David Javelosa. "Back then it was something that just didn't interest me, I was on the road, my gigs were paying my meals, and my label was paying my studio bill. Today, it's another part of my income."

"Never tell anyone who is making an offer what you want," advises manager Phil Frazier. "Ask them what they are offering. Usually it's around $1,000 up to $5,000 upfront, then royalties. Avoid giving up any publishing rights. If that's not possible, fight for a 50/50 split. Make damn sure the material has 'official' copyrights."

## Production Libraries

In order to get anywhere in this business, you need experience. Production music libraries are a good place to start. A production library houses a collection of songs that can be leased for a variety of purposes—commercials, videos, overseas markets, and so on. It's a lot like a warehouse filled with all different types of tunes for virtually every occasion. Producing songs for music libraries is a great way to learn the marketplace, and to gain exposure to the full range of music that is bought and sold every day.

"Doing work for music libraries is good for experience," confirms Jonathan Wolff. "You need the experience of doing all kinds of music. For the shows that I've worked on, every script is different. In one day I will have to record a piano concerto, Bluegrass music, an old school rap, and maybe some Dixieland. You've got to be able to do all of it. And a production library is a good place to really exercise those muscles."

Not only do you get the practice, the connections, and the credits, but you get a good income stream coming in from the music, and you own the songwriting royalties, meaning you're earning money through ASCAP, BMI, or SESAC whenever your cues are broadcast.

Entry-level composers should start working on that broadcast catalog. There are certain types of music that are global and timeless. If you're doing what's hot this week on the radio, well, maybe you'll get some placements this week, but it's not continuous. If you come up with a good package of news, suspense, and orchestral cues that are timeless, you're starting to generate royalty income that will sustain you.

# CONTINUING SATISFACTION:
## *Fat Cat Keeps* 𝄇
## *Getting Fatter*

My business, Mutato Muzika, lives up to some of the original desires from DEVO, when we talked about being a cooperative. Bob 1 and Bob 2 from DEVO are here every day. We see it as life after rock 'n' roll, a continuation of what we were doing because we get offered all of these odd, interesting jobs that have different demands.

—MARK MOTHERSBAUGH, FOUNDER
MUTATO MUZIKA, DEVO

*P*opular consensus has it that, in order to succeed in the music business, you need to stay true to your vision and surround yourself with people who are in sync with the goals you've set out to accomplish. You also have to stay smarter than your competition. This is business—it may be music, but it's still business—meaning, it runs on the bottom line. The music business is all about being strong and generating profits. Folks who've been in the business for awhile and say that they're into it because they like to play guitar, get high, and screw chicks have licked too much varnish, and haven't learned this business.

"I'm going to be turning thirty next year, and I realize that the fatigue of traveling and getting three hours' sleep in a different hotel every night, so I can do boring 'hanging and schmoozing' with radio and retail people, is definitely not for me," asserts Gregg Alexander, founder and destroyer of the platinum-selling pop act the New Radicals.

Life in the music business gets to be about more than girls and backstage passes. Once you've done that for a while, you need to feel that you're doing something with your life besides destroying brain cells and partying with your legions of dedicated fans. If you're at all motivated, you want to create your own little empire.

"I'm very happy with what I've accomplished with Century Media, which is based out of Europe," asserts Marco Barbieri. "I look back on when I started and we had a much smaller office that had no windows. There were four people working there. Century Media had one distributor and they only sold records in the United States. Now we've gotten distribution deals in Canada, South America, Mexico. We're responsible for the office in Australia, and we've done some deals in the Far East and Japan. We've grown to a staff of twenty-two people and two offices. We've built up a mail-order service that's doing remarkable business. When I stop and I look back on it, it is quite impressive."

The nice thing about aging in the business is that you gain wisdom, you grasp how the convoluted profit margin works, and you know how to put together the elements to build a successful business and/or career.

"When I first started at Century Media, we would be ecstatic if we got one tour a year, and now we usually have three tours going on simultaneously. We're getting bigger tours. It's a process of development," continues Marco. "Ultimately, that's what it's all about, finding good bands and nurturing them. It's the band and the label working together to try and make people's dreams come true."

## Family Matters

There are many aspects of the music business—management, touring, and so on—that keep you away from your family and keep you from settling down. Also, people in the music business don't make a ton of money early on, yet they devote 95 percent of their time to getting established. In the early stages, the music biz is a difficult and lonely place. It isn't until after you've been doing it awhile that it becomes a really satisfying venture.

"When I was twenty-five I sacrificed everything to become a rock star," notes manager/producer JJ French. "You're not having a stable relationship with your girl because your band is always in front of that. Your family relations are tough because your band is in front of that. Back when Twisted Sister was happening, I was probably unhappy most of the time because I was obsessed with the band."

And even if you become a rock star, unless you happen to be fortunate enough to be Elton John or the Stones, your fame is not going to last long anyway. Your personal relationships will continue on long after your

commercial popularity has peaked. So surround yourself with good people—both personally and professionally.

"In my run with Van Halen, we sold about 48 million albums, in the
Van Hagar era. I'm really happy to have been part of all that.
Unfortunately, after our manager Ed Leffler died, it all fell apart," notes
former Van Halen vocalist Sammy Hagar, now a solo artist. "Trying to find
another manager to replace Ed Leffler was impossible, so I didn't even try
to do that."

"I have incredible support from my wife," songwriter and producer
Gary Nicholson says effusively. "When she married me, she knew I was
going to be a musician. I made a living—not much of a living—I could
have probably made more of a living working a trash route. But she taught
school and I played guitar in nightclubs. Since we moved to Nashville, she
hasn't had to work to bring in money, but she's been carrying way more of
the workload of raising children than me, so I was allowed to work a lot
harder at songwriting. That's an incredible thing to have someone as your
partner who will share your dream and believe in you to the point where
they never even consider suggesting that you get a day job."

## New Ways to Get Your Kicks

After you've been in the business for awhile, there comes a time when
you'll want to reinvent yourself. It's a natural evolution: You move beyond
management to marketing, you take the elevator up from the street team
to marketing and promotion, from band to solo artist. If you've been in
the music business for a few years, you naturally evolve to find the position that's most comfortable for you.

"I like producing bands," declares JJ French. "Back when I was
twenty-five, I wanted to be playing in one. Now I've evolved and I enjoy
producing them. I imagine I could wind up as a record executive. But my
focus is not to be the live performer anymore."

For some, this evolution comes sooner than for others. Gregg
Alexander only needed to achieve one-hit-wonder status with his band,
the New Radicals, when he decided that he wanted to focus on producing
and writing songs for established acts as well as new artists. So Gregg folded the New Radicals and started up a production company to release
records on a variety of labels.

"It was an experience playing the artist, but I accomplished all of my
goals with this record, and I'm ready to move on and make the next step
in my career," confirms Gregg. "I've been writing songs for and working
with artists as varied as R&B acts to Belinda Carlisle intermittently for the
last nine years, and I'm looking forward to starting the day-to-day creative

process of building a successful production company. I view myself much the same as a just-getting-started Babyface or Matthew Wilder [No Doubt producer], who dabbled in performing, but whose real calling was being a producer."

Don't know if it's midlife or midcareer crisis, or just the need to do something completely different, but many music industry veterans like to diversify, even if it's something much more subtle, like switching the musical genre they're normally associated with. When the San Francisco Symphony and Metallica got together for a two-hour performance of heavy metal, the *San Francisco Chronicle* called the concert "a rollicking success."

Not to be outdone, crossover classical artist Yo-Yo Ma has been jamming with country fiddlers. Former pop idol Michael Bolton is singing opera arias. And who could forget the incredible Aretha Franklin being invited to perform with opera's Three Tenors? R&B's most notable diva is also studying classical piano at Juilliard.

Other musicians are venturing into different areas of marketing and merchandising to their young adult audience. A doll resembling pop sensation Brandy is on toy-store shelves, right near the Ozzy Osbourne action figure. For the five members of Aerosmith, who have sold more than 80 million records, a new thrill has been working on the Rock 'n' Roller Coaster at Disney–MGM Studios in Orlando. The indoor roller coaster features a high-speed launch from 0 to 60 miles per hour in 2.8 seconds, three inversions, rock-concert lighting, and a specially created Aerosmith soundtrack blasting from 120 onboard speakers in each car.

"When you've toured the world as much as we have, it's a real thrill to find a new audience," declares Aerosmith lead singer Steven Tyler. "Coming up with a soundtrack for this Disney ride really brought the kid out in all of us and has given us the opportunity to play audio gymnastics with our music."

## Your Own Satisfaction

The only thing predictable about the music business is that it's not predictable. Nobody's career path is the same, and nothing turns out quite as it was planned.

"To date, my career has been a real success, and everything's been a lot of fun," notes Jim Heath, frontman for the Reverend Horton Heat. "But, nothing's really turned out like I thought it would. I figured if I wrote good songs and I played good guitar and the band had a really kick-ass live show, that record company would be all over us. Instead, they were scared. We were passed over by every label in the book. I figured the cream would rise to the top, but life isn't always fair. But the way everything's worked out has been perfect, I really couldn't be happier."

Doesn't matter if you're in charge of the stock in the local Tower Records store, the president of your own record label, or anywhere in between. What's key is that you're enjoying your work and that you always find it exciting.

"We still have goals," asserts Earl Falconer of UB40, a Top 40 reggae band with a twenty-year career and millions of albums sold. "We can't say we've cracked everywhere in the world. We could still do better in America, for instance."

To keep it fresh and exciting, the members of UB40 all make music outside of the band. Vocalist Ali Campbel and saxophone player Brian Travers have a reggae label called Rockabessa Records, which is run out of Jamaica. James Brown, the drummer, has a live band that plays drum and bass, UB40 tunes, and some dance stuff. Earl is president of 175 BPM, a drum and bass music label in England.

"I've had different labels that I've done over the years, like drum and bass labels. I'm doing this one on my own. 175 BPM is a new thing, but obviously I really love that type of music—I'm a bass player," offers Earl. "When the UBs aren't working, the members are always working on their own."

After you've been in the business awhile, a lot of people get their jollies by diversifying into others areas. Some expand their knowledge in their chosen specialization or, after they've specialized, they realize that some parts of the business are a lot more enjoyable for them than others.

"Being a manager is like being a dad or a mom," insists Bob Chiappardi of Concrete Marketing. "Being a marketing guy is like being an uncle. Bands love my ass, just because they can come over. There are twenty-seven people at the office, they take photos, they raid the closet, they get CDs, chat, talk about the future. They spend the day, they leave with really big smiles on their face, and they think Concrete is really cool."

Those who are happy in their positions grow by taking on more complex responsibilities as their careers evolve, and what was once complex becomes simple.

"One of the parts of my job that I enjoy is the diversity of BMI," says Hanna Bolte. "We have many different departments that rely on media relations/corporate relations to help promote the programs that fall within those areas. From the Internet, licensing, film music, television composers, showcases, scholarships, workshops, panels, community events, there is always something different to work on. It's satisfying and challenging to work with so many varied areas all the time."

Even musicians who take jobs somewhat out of the musical mainstream find that professional gratification adds to their music. Maybe they didn't get the big royalties when it was their fifteen minutes, but they also haven't been burned out and compromised by the business. They've kept their perception and sensibility intact as a result of not touring their brains out and becoming rock stars.

"As I move more toward technology evangelism and working on the hardware side, I find it gives me more creative time for music of my own creative statement," notes composer and Yamaha technical evangelist David Javelosa. "That's very satisfying. For me, success as a musician is to have the means to satisfy one's imagination. Successful musicians have fulfilled the requirements of their musical goals and they can take their art and find the appropriate audience."

David has the satisfaction of sharing his music with others through writing music video games, and through playing the occasional musical event.

"I don't really like playing in bars, but I like to produce musical events," David says. "Chamber recitals, the occasional wedding, the occasional club appearance—I treat them not as part of a tour but as individual happenings, performance pieces. It's fun to play in front of people, but it's a drag to haul the equipment. It's a drag to deal with logistics the moment they cross into being anything near complex. Given the right audience, the minimum amount of gear and hassle, it can be a very enjoyable experience."

## Wisdom of the Aging

Everyone who was in the business in their teens and their twenties had great fun, but as they've matured, become parents, and developed publishing catalogs, they've become more responsible, something closer to regular adults. A maturing musician has to keep an eye on longevity, and make decisions in the best interest of everyone in the band.

"My sole responsibility is myself and the band members," notes Megadeth founder Dave Mustaine. "Whenever I go and I negotiate with management or agents or the record company, it's not just me taking care of me and my monkey on my back—I've got a wife and kids, David Ellefson and his wife and his kids, Jimmy de Grasso and his significant other, and Marty Friedman and his wife and his kids. So, I'm like an elder for a young town and I have to go in there and protect us and make sure I don't give away all of our stone soup."

You can't coast through the music business and expect it to become a career. It takes effort and direction. If you keep your long-term objectives in sight, you should become successful in your chosen area of endeavor.

# What Success Means

The nice thing about having such an abstract and varied business model as the music business is that success means different things to different people.

"The nicest thing about being in the music business is making enough money so that you can enjoy your family," notes JJ French. "I'm successful enough to enjoy the music with the people I like, and I'm able to spend quality time with my family."

David Javelosa observes, "I look at my current position in the hardware industry as a means of developing enough equity to have my own home studio complex, and continuing on with bigger, high-profile projects."

Career satisfaction means different things to different people. Make sure you know what you want and/or that you're open to opportunities.

# Sharing Your Music with Others

Once you've expanded beyond the stage, you still need the opportunity to make and share your music, since music, by its very nature, is meant to be shared with an audience. Some people still have a band, some just play at home. You'll find that as you become a more seasoned player, you'll come across an increasing number of musicians who share the same mindset as you do—musically you have that nonverbal communication ability—that most musicians ascribe to chemistry.

"These days, I look at performance as collaborative composition. I play with composers who have an understanding of compositional structure and the ability to create that in a real-time scenario," notes David Javelosa. "The people I like to play with are people who are capable of improvising along with me. Given the right audience, the minimum amount of gear and hassle, it can be a very enjoyable experience."

Others have simpler needs—they just want to play, with anybody, anywhere—as long as it's convenient. They are people who are always slutting around music circles.

"There are pockets of guitar circles where people get together in a folk tradition and turn the television off. They sit in the living room and play songs in big comfy chairs," points out engineer Bob Rice. "Old folk songs, Beach Boys songs, Kinks songs, Beatles songs, bluegrass music, country songs, George Jones songs, Grateful Dead songs, Paul Simon songs—just songwriters' stuff that everybody knows. When I can, I like to sit there and play mandolin, and that's great for me, because I get to solo all night long."

You find out about these musicians' gatherings through word of mouth, by being out there, and by networking. You go out, see music, meet people who play music, act interested in what they're doing, and voilà—you become a part of it.

"All I do is mess around with a guitar at the house—that's it," offers JJ French. "I just play for my daughter. I play, she runs around, she dances. She wants me to go to school with my guitar and play for her friends. I'm fine with that. I still buy electric guitars; I still collect them. I still love them. But I don't stand in front of a mirror waiting to be JJ French."

"I play four- and five-string fiddle, mandolin, various guitars—electric, acoustic, twelve-string. I play with the local musicians in my area once every couple months," notes Vince Castellucci. "I want to play more. I used to play almost eight hours a day every day, and almost every night, every afternoon, every evening."

Once your career evolves, music continues to be very satisfying. It just needs to be integrated into a more complete life.

"I learned a lot when I was with Van Halen," maintains Sammy Hagar. "I got a lot of musicianship knowledge. Eddie and Al are great musicians. Got a lot of platinum albums, a lot of number ones, and I got a lot of stage experience. I've always been a guitar player/singer, and to stand out there for 90 percent of the show, naked with the microphone, taught me how to be a better, more confident performer. I became a better singer, a better songwriter, a better musician, a better guitar player. I take all that with me as I venture further down the road."

## Down the Line

Do you have any idea what you're going to be doing ten years from now? Most people don't. They're just going with the flow, as long as the flow is good.

"I have no idea what my future will bring because I didn't think I'd be here right now, managing and producing Sevendust," chuckles JJ French. "Every day I think, 'Why am I still in this business?' I feel like Al Pacino in *The Godfather, Part III.* 'Just when I thought I was out, they sucked me back in.' I tried to leave the music business for awhile, but I got back into it and I love it. I anticipate that I'll be in it in some capacity for the rest of my working life."

"I wouldn't mind doing soundtracks, but for very specific movies," asserts David Javelosa. "I look at everything on a case-by-case basis. I wouldn't do a soundtrack just to do a soundtrack—it would have to be a meaningful project. I would love to score a science fiction movie."

Because this is such an ambiguous business, there is no single right and proper way to look at the unfolding of events and where it will lead you on your career path. Just like everybody else, you have something unique and specific that you would like to accomplish with your musical endeavors, and nobody but you knows what that is.

"The intention of my record label is to make money," affirms UB40's Earl Falconer. "It's not a real big market, but I want to try and do other people who are in my label's special kind of style. My goal is to introduce vocals and get some of it on the charts, but not water down the music side of it. As we make money, I'd like to develop bigger and better projects.

"Down the line, when I'm older, I'd like to do a bit of live work, and spend a fair amount of time in the recording studio," continues Earl. "That's one of the great things about being a musician. You just strive and try and get it perfect."

Musicians never get bored, because they can always do another take and make it sound better. It's the budget that dictates the limitations of the music. But there comes a point when you're doing it well enough, and you need to do something else to keep you excited.

For DEVO founder Mark Mothersbaugh, that excitement comes in the form of a new production company, established with Nancy Furgeson, called Atomika.

"My personal interest in the business had a lot to do with the fact that with music, you're at the very end of the production process, and a lot of time, you're problem solving. They say, 'That scene sucks, it doesn't have any energy, and we filmed it bad so you've got to fix it with the music,'" observes Mark Mothersbaugh. "At Atomika, we wanted to affect things and write the music earlier in the production process. That way we can open some of the doors that are already closed by the time a project gets to the music, which is considered an afterthought."

In the long run, all you get out of your work is personal satisfaction. If you make a good living and touch somebody's life, those are added bonuses. One of the most appealing aspects of the music business is that you can actually make somebody's life happier. What more could you want but to live well and spread happiness? There is no immortality. What do you want people to say about you long after you've disappeared from the music business?

"I'd like people to say that somehow I made a difference in their lives," concludes TV composer Jonathan Wolff. "Maybe I made them curious, and they weren't curious before. Maybe something I wrote helped them to relate to their loved one in a way that they wouldn't have before. Or that a song really meant something to somebody. I'd be really pleased to know that something I did could have the power to change somebody's life."

# *Bibliography* ‖:

## Section I. The Basics: Taking Care of Business

Laskow, Michael, "Gary Nicholson, Songwriting Producer," in *Taxi http://www.taxi.com/meters9901/insider9901.html* (accessed February 1999).

Laskow, Michael, "Jonathan Wolff, TV Composer," in *Taxi http://www.taxi.com/meters/insider9903.html* (accessed February 1999).

## Section II. Career Paths: Where It's At

### Chapter 5. Business Options: Mr. Pinstripe Suit

MIT, "The Small Catechism of Martin Luther Part One: The Ten Commandments," *http://www.mit.edu:8001/afs/athena.mit.edu/activity/l/lem/www/luther-catechism-1-decalogue.html* (accessed March 1999).

### Chapter 6. Your Own Business

Reece, Doug, "Q&A With Al Teller," in *MP3.com http://www.mp3.com/news/172.html*, February 19, 1998 (accessed January 1999).

Strauss, Neil, "Rap Revolutionaries Plan an Internet Release," in the *New York Times, http://search.nytimes.com/search/daily/bin/fastweb?getdoc+site+iib-site+84+0+wAAA+mp3*, April 16, 1999.

Williams, Geoff, "Going Indie: Spinning Your Own Record Label," in *Entrepreneur Magazine Online, http://www.entrepreneurmag.com/page.hts?N=7688*, April 1999 (accessed May 1999).

### Chapter 7. Selling Albums: Give It to Me Baby

Aswad, Jem, "ASCAP'S Music Business 101: A Conversation with Richard Gottehrer," in *ASCAP's Art & Commerce Café http://www.ascap.com/art-commerce/gottehrer.html* (accessed March 1999).

### Chapter 8. Turn Up the Radio

Erwin, Liz, "An Interview with Sheryl Stewart," in *The Communicator* *http://www.air1radio.com/sheryl2.html,* January 1999 (accessed March 1999).

Pollack, Marc, "King Biscuit Gravy for CAK," in *The Hollywood Reporter* *http://www.hollywoodreporter.com/,* June 11–13, 1999.

Santarelli, Vince, "Dan Ingram: The RadioDigest.com Interview," in *Radio Digest http://www.radiodigest.com/news/1999/nat_030399_ingram_1.htm* (accessed March 12, 1999).

DJ David X, "The DJ David X Book," *http://www.djdavidx.com/* (accessed February 1999).

Zoller Seitz, Matt, "An Inteview With Howard Stern: King of All Media," *The Star-Ledger http://www.nj.com/spotlight/stern/* (accessed January, 1999).

### Chapter 10. Production: Minute with the Maker

"Bedford Roadie Tommy Kotchik Interview," *http://www.geocities.com/ SunsetStrip/Venue/4544/roadie.html* (accessed February 1999).

Endino, Jack, "Jaq FAQ," *http://www.nwlink.com/~endino/faq.html* (accessed February 1999).

Jones, John, "What Does a Producer Have to Do with Making a Record?" *http://www.johnjones.com/comindex.html* (accessed February 1999).

Wheaton, Mark, "Patrick Adams Interview," *http://member.aol.com/ papmus/what.htm* (accessed February 1999).

### Chapter 11. On Tour: Wherever I May Roam

Kuenning, Karl, "Roadie: A True Story (at Least the Parts I Remember)," *http://www.roadie.net/howroad.htm,* 1998 (accessed February 1999).

### Chapter 12. Band Management: Won't Get Fooled Again

Berman, Anthony R., Esq. "Break on Through (to the Other Side): Talent Agencies and Artists—A Primer on Artist-Talent Agency Agreements," *http://www.ibslaw.com/melon/archive.html* 204 (2) (accessed February 1999).

Kidd, Tom, "25 Tips to Choosing the Right Manager," in *Music Connection* 5 (23) (March 1999), p. 28.

Morgan, Sloane, Esq. "Trouble Ahead, Trouble Behind (A Suggestion to the Entertainment Industry: Mediate)" *http://www.ibslaw.com/ melon/archive.html* 2 (210) (accessed February 1999).

"Services and Fees" in *Avotar, Inc., http://www.avotar.com/service.html* (accessed February 1999).

### Chapter 13. Booking and Promotion: Rock 'N' Roll All Night

Dawson, Mary, "Do-It-Yourself Music Publishing—Part I," in *Writer's Write http://www.writerswrite.com/journal/apr99/dawson.htm,* 1999 (accessed March 1999).

Drozdowski, Ted, "How One Man Is Gobbling Up the Nation's Concert Business—and What it Could Mean for You," in *The Boston Phoenix http://weeklywire.com/ww/03-23-98/boston_feature_1.html,* March 23, 1998 (accessed March 1999).

Harlan, James, Esq., "Intro to Music Publishing," *http://www.harlan-law.com/publications/intro_music_publishing.html* (accessed March 1999).

Hildegard Publishing Company, "About Us," *http://www.hildegard.com/* (accessed March 1999).

Marvelous Entertainment, "Your #1 Southeast U.S.A. Connection for the Best Bands for All Occasions!" *http://www.marvelousentertainment. com/bandhome.html* (accessed March 1999).

### Chapter 14. Entertainment Law: I Fought the Law and the Law Won

Laskow, Michael, "Donald Passman, Music Attorney, A&M Records," in *Taxi http://www.taxi.com/meters9901/insider9701.html* (accessed March 1999).

Morgan, Sloane, Esq., "Trouble Ahead, Trouble Behind (A Suggestion to the Entertainment Industry: Mediate)" *http://www.ibslaw.com/melon/ archive.html* 2 (210) (accessed February 1999).

### Chapter 17. The Web: Draw the Online

Digital Music Network, "MP3 Summit: Ice-T, Others Discuss Illegal MP3s," in *Webnoize http://www.webnoize.com,* June 16, 1999.

Mendel, Brett, "Music Industry Points the Way for Mainstream Digital Audio," in *Billboard Online Sites + Sounds http://www.billboard.com* (accessed May 31, 1999).

Payne, John, "The Rules of the Game: Robert Fripp on the Profession of Music," in *L.A. Weekly http://www.laweekly.com/* (accessed March 1999).

Philips, Chuck, "Veteran Industry Execs Will Head Start-Up Internet Record Company—Gary Gersh and John Silva Will Become Copresidents of DEN, Which Will Promote and Sell Recordings from its Web Site," in *The Los Angeles Times http://www.latimes.com/* (accessed June 1, 1999).

Pollack, Marc, "Ertegun Charms EAT'M Gathering," in *The Hollywood Reporter http://www.hollywoodreporter.com/,* May 21–23, 1999.

Reece, Doug, "Q&A With Al Teller," in *MP3.com http://www.mp3.com/ news/172.html,* February 19, 1998 (accessed March 1999).

Reid, Vernon, "Creativity and the Internet: 'Artist' or 'Content Provider'?" in *ASCAP's Art & Commerce Café http://www.ascap.com/*, 1999 (accessed March 1999).

Sullivan, Jennifer, "MP3: A Flash in the Pan," in *Wired http://www.wired.com/news/news/email/explode-infobeat/culture/story/19189.html* (accessed March 1999).

University of Cambridge, "Training Directory," *http://www.cam.ac.uk/CambUniv/TD/Management.html#title1*, 1999 (accessed March 1999).

## Section III. Paths for Musicians: The Long and Winding Road

### Chapter 18. Making Music for a Living: Further on Up the Road

The Associated Press, "Drumstick Maker Doing Well," in *The New York Times http://www.nytimes.com/aponline/f/AP-Profile-Drumstick-Plant.html* (accessed May 11, 1999).

### Chapter 19. Working for Hire: Get Out There

Brabec, Jeffrey and Todd, "Money, Success, and the Movies, Part I—Whether the Score is Dramatic, Soothing, Romantic, Comedic or Foreboding, It Is an Integral Part of the Fabric of any Motion Picture," in *ASCAP's Art & Commerce Café http://www.ascap.com/artcommerce/movies-part1.html*, 1999 (accessed March 1999).

Coleman, Calmetta, "Forget the Radio: Now Songs Become Smash Hits in Stores," *The Wall Street Journal http://www.wsj.com* (accessed July 9, 1999).

Fusilli, Jim, "Scoring Success for 'Star Wars,'" in *The Wall Street Journal, http://www.wsj.com*, 1999 (accessed February 1999).

Hettrick, Scott, "Bowie Changes Again, Goes PC," in *The Hollywood Reporter, http://www.hollywoodreporter.com/* (accessed May 12, 1999).

Laskow, Michael, "Gary Nicholson, Songwriting Producer," in *Taxi http://www.taxi.com/meters9901/insider9901.html* (accessed February 1999).

# *About the Author* ||:

*A*llow me to introduce myself, Jodi Summers, and my company, World View Media. We hang out with bands and create
feature stories. We do things like go on tour with Cibo Matto
and go in the studio with Metallica and then share it in writing with the world. Pretty cool job, huh? World View Media sells these
stories, articles, and graphics to magazines, newspapers, Web sites, and
online services throughout the world. Our current clientele includes
more than 150 college newspapers in the United States and 40 publications worldwide.

Online, World View Media has created content for *www.makeitmu-
sic.net, www.cyberpop.com, www.mp3.com, www.emusic.com,* and *www.iln.net,*
among others. We managed the development and launch of *www.film-
zone.com, www.sweetstuff.com,* and *www.stonejungle.com* and we constantly
contribute content to sites too numerous to mention through their syndi-
cations. Take a look: You'll find comprehensive features on things like "The
Korn School of Music," comprehensive "Star Wars" entertainment, and
"Rock Around the Web."

A unique benefit World View Media offers is genre-specific, e-mail
databases and communities that permit us to better market and promote
our clients. If your target market consists of music-oriented individuals
from 12 to 40, we can help you better reach them.

I serve as U.S. correspondent for German publications *Net Investor,
Blickpunkt: Film, Connect, Multimedia,* and *Interaktiv,* and am associate
editor for *Hit Parader* magazine in the United States. My stories have
appeared in such publications as *Wired, Electronic Entertainment, Music*

*Computers, Rolling Stone, Hollywood Reporter, Esquire,* and *People.*
*Domestically,* I have been on the editorial staff of *Hit Parader, Rockbeat,*
*Rip, Faces, Rolling Stone, Penthouse,* and *Wrestling 2000,* as well as a U.S.
correspondent for various international publications, including Japan's
*Tokyo Today, Viva Rock,* and *Crossroads.*

I have written three music self-help books: *The Interactive Music*
*Handbook, Making and Marketing Music: A Musician's Guide to Financing,*
*Promoting and Distributing Your Album,* and this one, *Moving Up In the*
*Music Business.* I am currently writing a book called *Making Music Online.*

I can be reached at *cgoddess@compuserve.com.*

# Index

# Books from Allworth Press

**Making and Marketing Music: The Musician's Guide to Financing, Distributing, and Promoting Albums** by Jodi Summers (softcover, 6 × 9, 240 pages, $18.95)

**The Interactive Music Handbook: The Definitive Guide to Internet Music Strategies, Enhanced CD Production, and Business Development** by Jodi Summers (softcover, 6 × 9, 296 pages, $19.95)

**Creative Careers in Music** by Josquin des Pres and Mark Landsman (softcover, 6 × 9, 224 pages, $18.95)

**The Songwriter's and Musician's Guide to Nashville, Revised Edition** by Sherry Bond (softcover, 6 × 9, 224 pages, $18.95)

**Making It in the Music Business: The Business and Legal Guide for Songwriters and Performers, Revised Edition** by Lee Wilson (softcover, 6 × 9, 288 pages, $18.95)

**How to Pitch and Promote Your Songs, Revised Edition** by Fred Koller (softcover, 6 × 9, 192 pages, $19.95)

**The Copyright Guide: A Friendly Guide to Protecting and Profiting from Copyrights, Revised Edition** by Lee Wilson (softcover, 6 × 9, 192 pages, $19.95)

**The Trademark Guide: A Friendly Guide For Protecting and Profiting from Trademarks** by Lee Wilson (softcover, 6 × 9, 192 pages, $18.95)

**Booking and Tour Management for the Performing Arts** by Rena Shagan (softcover, 6 × 9, 272 pages, $19.95)

**Technical Theatre for Nontechnical People** by Drew Campbell (softcover, 6 × 9, 256 pages, $18.95)

**Artists Communities: A Directory of Residencies in the United States That Offer Time and Space for Creativity, Second Edition** by the Alliance of Artists' Communities (softover, 6¾ × 10, 240 pages, $18.95)

Please write to request our free catalog. To order by credit card, call 1-800-491-2808 or send a check or money order to Allworth Press. 10 East 23rd Street, Suite 510, New York, NY 10010. Include $5 for shipping and handling for the first book ordered and $1 for each additional book. Ten dollars plus $1 for each additional book if ordering from Canada. New York State residents must add sales tax.

To see our complete catalog on the World Wide Web, or to order online, you can find us at *www.allworth.com*.